Authentic Christianity

examples & application
Know about God
" of "

Discovery House Publishers

Books, music, and videos that feed the soul with the Word of God

Box 3566 Grand Rapids, MI 49501

About sharing the good news—
It's one beggar telling another where to
find bread.

Authentic
Christianity

The Classic Bestseller
on Living the Life
of Faith with Integrity

The glass is always half full
Christ always triumphs - all things His glory
Impact is unmistakable
Integrity always apparent
Evidence/results only explainable by God at work

Ray C. Stedman

Discovery House Publishers is affiliated with RBC Ministries, Grand Rapids, Michigan 49512.

Discovery House books are distributed to the trade exclusively by Barbour Publishing, Inc., Uhrichsville, Ohio 44683.

Unless otherwise noted, all Scripture quotations are taken from the HOLY BIBLE: NEW INTERNATIONAL VERSION. © 1973, 1978, 1984 International Bible Society. Used by permission of Zondervan Publishing House.

Library of Congress Cataloging-in-Publication Data

Stedman, Ray C.
  Authentic Christianity : the classic bestseller on living the life of faith with integrity / by Ray C. Stedman.
      p.   cm.
  Previously published: Waco, Tex. : Word Books, 1975.

  ISBN 1-57293-017-9

  1. Christian life. I. Title.
BV4501.2.S738   1996
248.4—dc20
                                                96-22610
                                                CIP

Printed in the United States of America

00 01 02 /CHG/ 10 9 8 7 6 5

To Elaine
loyal helper, loving critic,
a woman to be proud of.

CONTENTS

PREFACE

THIS IS THE BOOK I have wanted to write above all others. It deals with the very heart of the gospel, the most important truth contained in the pages of Scripture. That truth is the new covenant of which the Lord Jesus spoke when He passed the cup at the Last Supper and said, "This is the blood of the new covenant which is shed for many for the forgiveness of sins."

When we understand the full implications of that new covenant, we discover the most liberating secret in the Word of God! It is the secret, as Paul put it, of "Christ in you, the hope of glory." All of God's plans for present victory over evil, and all His plans for future glory rest squarely on the amazing fact of our fundamental union with Christ!

I pray that God will use this book to lead you into a deeper, richer experience of this central truth of the Christian life, and that He will enable you to fully discover the glorious liberty of being a child of God! I pray that this book will help you to move beyond religion, beyond doctrines, beyond rules, beyond rituals, and into that life-changing experience of being intimately connected with Christ at the very core of your being—for *that* is authentic Christianity!

Ray C. Stedman

1

The Great Imitation

HIS CLASSMATES CALLED HIM "the Dumb Ox" because he was heavyset, serious, and usually silent. Historians, however, call him "the Angelic Doctor," and Roman Catholics revere him as a saint. His name: Thomas Aquinas—the most influential theologian of the thirteenth century.

If the young scholar's mother could have had her way, the world would never have heard of Thomas Aquinas. She strongly opposed his wishes to study theology and join a priestly order. In fact, she even had him confined in a castle for over a year in an attempt to keep him from becoming a priest.

The life mission of Thomas Aquinas was to reconcile the Christian faith with human reason, and to intellectually prove the existence of God. Of the many theological books Aquinas wrote, his final work—the *Summa Theologica* or *Summary Treatise of Theology* (1265–73)—is considered his greatest and most important. Amazingly, Aquinas himself never finished the *Summa Theologica*. No, he didn't die before it could be completed. He simply lost interest and stopped writing!

What happened to Aquinas that made him abruptly abandon his lifelong pursuit of theology? We find a clue in the fact that his great unfinished work was composed of three parts: "On God," "The Moral Life of Man," and "On Christ." He had completed the first two sections and was deep into the writing of the final section on Christ when something happened to him—a profound and emotionally shattering spiritual experience. Aquinas himself was never able to put that life-changing experience into words, but many who have studied his life believe that, in the process of writing about Christ and meditating on our Lord's life and words, Aquinas experienced a vision in which he came face to face with the Savior.

Following his spiritual encounter with Jesus, Aquinas said, "I have seen that which makes all I have written and taught look small to me. My writing days are over." And with that, he simply stopped writing, leaving unfinished his theological masterpiece on Christ. All human pursuits—even the study of religion and theology—are mere pale imitations once we come into the presence of the Great Reality, Jesus Himself.

The Christian life begins with an encounter with Jesus Christ. It cannot be otherwise. "He who has the Son has life; he who does not have the Son of God does not have life" (1 John 5:12). Many influences and experiences may lead us to an encounter with Jesus Christ. Those influences and experiences may even be intensely religious and theologically profound—but until a person responds to the promise of Christ and receives Him as Lord, there can be no spiritual reality, no eternal life.

12   **Authentic Christianity**

The act of receiving Christ may be so effortless, gentle, and gradual that the person may not even be aware of the exact moment he or she passed from death into life. This is often the case with children who are raised from an early age to love and follow Jesus. In other cases, the moment of conversion is shattering and dramatic, as in the spiritual experience of Thomas Aquinas or the conversion of Paul on the road to Damascus. In still other cases, a specific moment of decision results in the conversion experience—yet it takes place without great drama, miracles, emotions, or visions; that is the conversion experience John Wesley describes when he says he felt "strangely warmed" when he gave his life to Christ.

In still other cases, conversion may actually be a tortuous, painful experience, accompanied with great resistance, almost as if the individual is "dragged kicking and screaming" into the kingdom of God; such was the case with St. Augustine. He had spent years seeking pleasure and exploring various worldly philosophies until one day he heard a voice, like that of a child, repeating, "Take up and read." Believing this to be a command from God to read the Bible, Augustine randomly opened to the book of Romans and read, "clothe yourselves with the Lord Jesus Christ, and do not think about how to gratify the desires of the sinful nature" (Romans 13:14). Though he did not want to give up his sinful ways, though he resisted God's call upon his life, Augustine knew that he had at last discovered the truth—and he gave up the struggle and accepted Jesus Christ as Savior and Lord.

A person's encounter with Jesus Christ—what we call "conversion"—may take place in any one of a number of ways. However the act of conversion occurs, it is essential before one can live the authentic Christian life.

No other way

The experience of encountering Christ rests upon the written promises of the Bible. At least some experience of the truth of God's Word is essential to believing in or receiving Christ. It is the biblical account of the crucifixion and resurrection of Jesus which gives us reason to believe that Jesus is alive and available to us; that Jesus can, by the Holy Spirit, actually come to live within a human being; and that He can so entwine His life with our own that, from then on, we and Christ can be essentially regarded as one. The biblical account of Jesus' life and character gives us the basis for believing that Jesus truly is the Savior He claimed to be and that He has the power to set us free from bondage to sin. Our assurance as Christians rests upon such promises as, "Come to me, all you who are weary and burdened, and I will give you rest" (Matthew 11:28) and "I am the light of the world. Whoever follows me will never walk in darkness, but will have the light of life" (John 8:12).

But no matter how clearly we may understand who Jesus is and what He can do in our lives, and even how He gives us eternal life (by His death and resurrection, God's plan of salvation), we cannot receive the gift of eternal life until we, in our human will, respond to the invitation of Jesus and choose to receive Him, obey Him, and follow Him. God's plan of salvation, as it is presented to us throughout the New Testament, is aimed squarely at our human will, our human decision-making ability. We must make a choice to surrender to the lordship of Jesus.

We cannot attain eternal life through a mere intellectual exercise. We do not become authentic Christians by intellectually comprehending and accepting the historical facts about Jesus. Nor do we become authentic Christians by grasping the theological implications of His death and resurrection. We do not become authentic Christians by adhering to certain moral and ethical standards that Jesus taught. Nor do we become authentic Christians by trying to relate to God apart from Jesus Christ. Our lives must be joined to His life. We become authentic Christians by asking Jesus to come in as Lord and Master, and by trusting Him to accomplish and fulfill His eternal life in us by means of the Holy Spirit. When that happens, a miracle takes place—even though that miracle may be of a quiet, almost invisible kind. A new quality of life—*eternal* life—is imparted to us and we are "made alive in Christ." It is this divine action that makes us authentic Christians. Nothing else can do it. "He who has the Son has life; he who does not have the Son of God does not have life." It is that simple.

Signs of life

Conversion is just the beginning. A newborn baby, fresh from her mother's womb, is a complete, authentic person, a genuine human being, even though she is physically and mentally undeveloped. In the same way, a newborn Christian is a complete, authentic Christian and truly shares the life of Christ, even though he is spiritually undeveloped. There is much to be learned and experienced before this person achieves anything that can properly be called maturity. Happily, however, certain manifestations of the new life do quickly appear. Perhaps the easiest to recognize is a sense of peace and well-being, especially in terms of one's feelings about God. It is, as Paul tells us, the result of God's Spirit bearing witness with our human spirit that we are now the children of God (see Romans 8:16). And that sense of peace is made more intense and lasting as we come to realize the full implication of having our sin forgiven through our relationship with Christ. This release from guilt and shame is a large part of the peace Christians experience.

One of the joys of a new Christian is a new and exciting sense of belonging to a family. We discover we are not alone, but have become members of a large and ever-growing family. As members of that family, we have many brothers and sisters to relate to and enjoy, while having continual access to our heavenly Father through prayer and the presence of the Holy Spirit. For many, the most joyful aspect of this new life is release from the fear of death and what lies beyond. To have the certain hope of heaven rather than the fear of hell is a relief beyond our ability to express.

Because of these elements of the Christian life, many new Christians experience intense excitement and joy. The Bible becomes a fresh and exciting book, and meeting with other Christians is a continual joy. The change that comes over the outlook and emotions of the new Christian is obvious to everyone. Many new believers wonder, *Why did I wait so long to experience something so wonderful?*

Three possible choices

This initial state of euphoria may continue for weeks or even months. Inevitably, sooner or later, the old natural life begins to reassert itself. The glow begins to fade from Christian worship, and Bible reading becomes less and less rewarding. Christian fellowship in meetings and individual contact becomes dull and routine. Old patterns of thinking and behavior begin to reassert themselves. This is a critical time when one of three possibilities may occur.

First, the young Christian may continue his decline to the point of dropping out of all Christian relationships, neglecting the Bible, abandoning prayer, losing interest in spiritual things, and falling back into his pre-Christian lifestyle. This may be just a temporary period of "backsliding," one of several periods of remission before the person settles into a consistent Christian lifestyle. In the majority of cases, however, there is no return (at least for many years). The question naturally occurs: Was this person ever really a Christian at all?

Second, the young Christian may become aware of his cold and rebellious heart, become frightened by the thought of regressing to what he was before, and repentantly cast himself upon God's mercy, renewing his trust in God's promises. Such Christians often seek the help of older, more experienced Christians as mentors and prayer partners who encourage them and hold them accountable as they return to a state of obedience, peace, and joy. This cycle may be repeated many times until it becomes habitual and he comes to think of it as normal Christianity. On the other hand he may, happily, learn something from each repeated cycle, so that his eyes are opened to the truth and he is able to leave his spiritual roller-coaster existence and become a stable, mature, Spirit-led Christian.

The third and most likely possibility is that the new Christian may discover what millions of others before him have learned: It is possible to avoid the pain and humiliation of these cycles of repentance and renewal by maintaining an outward facade of spiritual commitment, moral impeccability, and orthodox behavior. One can simply maintain an outward reputation for spiritual maturity that is satisfying to the ego, even though he is inwardly haunted by the fact that his "Christianity" is a hollow shell. Such an outwardly Christian life-style is so prevalent today that a new Christian can hardly be blamed for adopting it and regarding it as normal. He drifts into it with only an occasional twinge of doubt or a rare, faint pang of conscience.

He is in denial, and would be deeply offended if anyone called him what he really is: a hypocrite. To him, the word *hypocrite* suggests something nasty and sinister, like the Pharisees of old. He sees himself as a "real Christian," even though his faith is only an inch deep. It is not the kind of rock-solid, deep-rooted relationship with Jesus that can carry him through any crisis. The fact is, the "peace" he claims to have is present only while his circumstances are untroubled; when his circumstances turn dark and troubling, his "peace" evaporates instantly. The "joy" he sings about seldom shows on his face, and the "Christian love" he is talks about is reserved only for those who please him and get along with him. It is all a giant (though largely unconscious) sham. He may be a true Christian in whose heart Christ dwells, but he does not live the Christian life on a consistent basis. He may be a highly moral, highly religious, even a highly generous person—but the reality is that he is living pretty much as he did before his conversion, only now his speech and behavior are covered with a thin glaze of Christianity. That glaze is the first thing to crack and crumble when life becomes irritating, difficult, or threatening.

The phony and the genuine

You may think this is a harsh judgment. Many people think that the mark of an authentic Christian is doctrinal purity; that a person is a Christian whose beliefs are biblical and doctrinally orthodox. People who equate orthodoxy with authenticity find it hard to even consider the possibility that, despite the correctness of all their doctrinal positions, they may have missed the deepest reality of the authentic Christian life. But we must never forget that true Christianity is more than teaching—it is a *way of life*. In fact, it is *life itself*. "He who has the Son has life," remember? When we talk about life, we are talking about something that is far more than mere morality, far more than doctrinal accuracy. Life is a positive quality, not negative—a description of what we fundamentally *are*, not what we are not. The eternal life that Jesus brings to us is radical, not superficial. It is humble, not self-promoting. It is compassionate, not indifferent. It is courageous, not timid or retiring. It is a far cry indeed from the mild compatibility, agreeability, and affability that passes for Christianity in thousands of churches across the land. In fact, the Great Imitation is so widely accepted as genuine Christianity that the real thing is often regarded as a threat or a heresy whenever it appears.

Our purpose in this book is to trace the sharp distinctions between the phony and the genuine. We shall be guided entirely by the revelation of Scripture, for the Word of God is the only sufficient guide to distinguish truth from error. We shall explore together a major passage from Paul's epistles—2 Corinthians 2:14 to 6:13. In this passage Paul helps the Corinthians to distinguish between authentic Christianity, as he himself lived it, and the pale imitation that many of them had mistaken for the real thing. Then the apostle takes them (and us with them), step by step into an understanding of the enormous enrichment that awaits those who learn to live by the new covenant, which gives life, rather than the old covenant, which kills. Our study of this passage will not be "theological" (that is, lofty, complicated, and technical), nor will it be "devotional" (horrible word). Rather, it will be intensely practical and straightforward. Our goal in this book is to rediscover the kind of genuine, workable Christianity that can be put to the test in the trenches of everyday living—the kind of Christianity that can bring you safely through any crisis, that will enable you to look back on your life and say, "I have truly known God."

If you are interested in that kind of real, radical, authentic Christianity, read on.

II

The Real Thing

IT HAS ALWAYS SEEMED UNFAIR to me that many churches (and some individual Christians) keep careful records on how many converts they make to Christianity, but never keep any record of how many they drive away from Christ! Fairness would seem to dictate that both sides of the ledger should be maintained! The fact is, many churches turn far more people from Christ than they ever win to Him—and frequently the most zealous and orthodox Christians are the very ones who drive the most people away! The reason, as we have seen, is that while they may indeed be true Christians themselves, the life manifest is false Christianity—as phony as a three-dollar bill.

True, there is a false Christianity that is practiced by those who aren't Christians at all. There are many religious frauds who have *never* been real Christians, and there are apostates who give every appearance of being Christian for awhile, then abandon the whole thing. But surely the most subtle stratagem ever devised by Satan to deceive and mislead people is that of causing genuine Christians to practice a sham

Christianity before the world. You can't detect and guard against this kind of sham Christianity by making people sign a doctrinal statement or by having them recite a creed. This type of phony Christianity is always orthodox. It is frequently very zealous and feeds upon consecration services and dedication meetings. It uses all the right terms and behaves in the proper, orthodox manner, but the net result is that it repels people from Christ rather than attracting people to Christ.

In sharp contrast to this is the Real Thing—authentic Christianity as its founder, Jesus Christ Himself, intended it to be. Authentic Christianity never needs advertisement or publicity. It gives off a fragrance and a fascination that attracts people like flies are attracted to honey. Is *everyone* attracted to authentic Christianity? Absolutely not! Many people are antagonized and even outraged when they discover what Christianity is truly about. But in general, the initial character of authentic Christianity is one that attracts crowds and compels admiration.

The Christianity of Jesus and Paul

There is, of course, no clearer demonstration of real Christianity than Christ Himself. Today, there are many varieties of Christianity, but the most attractive form of Christianity of all is the *original*—the Christianity of Jesus Christ. This was the authentic Christian life in its purest, most consistent form. Many people have a problem understanding, applying, and identifying with the Christianity of Jesus because they feel He, being the Son of God, had an edge over the rest of us. "Not fair, comparing me to Jesus!" they protest. "Sure, Jesus was undoubtedly human—but He was also God. From His divine side, He drew supernatural power to resist evil and achieve great things in a way I could never do."

Yes, Jesus was fully God—but we must never forget that He was also fully human, with all the limitations that go with our humanity. We *can* live our lives as He lived His. We *can* base our lives on the model He has set before us. This is practical, livable truth, and the Scriptures are very clear on this point. Here are a few passages which commend Jesus to us as an example we *can* and *should* follow on a practical, daily basis:

> Because he himself suffered when he was tempted, he is able to help those who are being tempted (Hebrews 2:18).

> We do not have a high priest who is unable to sympathize with our weaknesses, but we have one who has been tempted in every way, just as we are—yet was without sin (Hebrews 4:15).

> To this you were called, because Christ suffered for you, leaving you an example, that you should follow in his steps (1 Peter 2:21).

How is this possible? How can we hope to pattern our lives after the life of a perfect Person who was God in the flesh? Isn't that like trying to high-jump the Empire State Building or broad-jump the Pacific Ocean? Isn't that asking the impossible? Well, yes and no. Yes, it is impossible for us to live perfect, sinless lives, but no, it is not impossible for us to set a *goal* of Christlikeness. Every time we fail in our pursuit of that goal, we simply go back to God for forgiveness and restoration, and He puts us back on the road to our goal once again. The key principle is found in Philippians 2:5–8, which I've quoted here from the New Revised Standard Version (emphasis added):

Let the same mind be in you that was in Christ Jesus, who, though he was in the form of God, did not regard equality with God as something to be exploited, but *emptied himself*, taking the form of a slave, being born in human likeness. And being found in human form, he humbled himself and became obedient to the point of death—even death on a cross.

Note that key phrase: *Jesus emptied Himself!* He set aside the prerogatives and powers of Godhood in order to identify fully with us. He lived the same kind of life we live, facing temptation, suffering pain and sorrow, enduring frustration, just as we do. He approached life the same way you and I must approach life: living in dependence on God the Father, seeking guidance and strength through continual prayer, trusting God and listening to His leading, and being humbly obedient— "not my will, but yours." That is why we are to "let the same mind be in [us] that was in Christ Jesus" (NRSV). That is authentic Christianity, the Christianity of Christ, Christianity in its truest, purest, most distilled form. That is the Christianity which you and I are to follow, the only Christianity worthy of the name.

The apostle Paul lived his life by the same principle, patterning his life after the example of Christ. In 1 Corinthians 11:1, he writes, "Follow my example, *as I follow the example of Christ*" (emphasis added). That is why the apostle's ministry was so attractive to the people around him. That is why his preaching was so effective in changing hearts and minds. He was an imitator of Christ. As we examine a selection from Paul's second letter to the Christians at Corinth—one of the most biographical of all Paul's letters—we will gain insight into Paul's own experiences as an imitator of

Christ and of His ministry. There, Paul reveals to us in the clearest terms the secret of his own great ministry.

Since authentic Christianity is the goal of Scripture, there are many passages in both the Old and New Testaments that could be used to guide us to this end. But we shall choose one particular selection from Paul's second letter to the Christians at Corinth. This letter is one of the most biographical of all Paul's letters. In it the apostle gives us insight into his own experiences and reveals to us in the clearest terms the secret of his great ministry.

The first one and one-half chapters of 2 Corinthians indicate that Paul was being challenged by certain Christians at Corinth. They had been affected by some Jewish Christians from Jerusalem who suggested that Paul was not a genuine apostle at all because (1) he was not one of the original twelve, and (2) some of his teachings went beyond the law of Moses. Claiming he was not a real apostle, they insisted his brand of Christianity was not real Christianity. One of the devil's favorite tricks is to brand the truth as a big lie, and that's exactly what was happening at Corinth.

Five unmistakable marks

Paul's response to these charges is to describe for us the nature of his ministry. As we shall see, Paul's ministry bears five unmistakable qualities of Christianity that cannot be successfully counterfeited. These qualities have nothing to do with personality or temperament, so anyone who discovers the secret of authentic Christianity can attain them. They are timeless, so they are just as genuine in the twenty-first century as in the first.

We begin our journey of discovery in 2 Corinthians 2:14. In this verse, we find the first three marks of authentic Christianity (the remaining two qualities are found in the verses that follow): "Thanks be to God, who always leads us in triumphal procession in Christ and through us spreads everywhere the fragrance of the knowledge of him" (2 Corinthians 2:14). Let's examine the marks of authentic Christianity, one by one.

Mark No. 1: Unquenchable optimism

The first mark is found in the very first phrase: "Thanks be to God." One unmistakable evidence of radical Christianity is a spirit of thankfulness, even amid trial and difficulty. It is a kind of *unquenchable optimism.* The world operates by the gloomy principle of Murphy's Law: Whatever can go wrong, will go wrong. Authentic Christians operate by a belief in God's grace, love, and ultimate control. You can see the unquenchable optimism of authentic Christianity clearly in the book of Acts, where a note of triumph resounds throughout despite all the dangers, hardships, persecutions, pressures, and perils that the early Christians experienced. The same continual note of thanksgiving is reflected in all of Paul's letters as well as those of John, Peter, and James.

The attitude of thanksgiving evident in these passages is genuine and profound. There is nothing artificial about it. It is a far cry from the imitation thanksgiving often seen in Christians today. Some people think they are expected to repeat pious and thankful words, even when they don't feel thankful. They assume that's the way Christians are supposed to act. Many have settled for a form of Christian stoicism, a grin-and-bear-it attitude which even a non-Christian can adopt when there's nothing much he can do about a situation. But that is a long way from true Christian thankfulness. To listen to some Christians today, you would think God expects us to screw on a smile and go around saying, "Hallelujah, I've got cancer!" That's not what our unquenchable optimism is all about.

Authentic Christianity is rooted in reality. It feels all the hurt and pain of adverse circumstances, and does not find any pleasure in them. But authentic Christianity does see the result being produced—not only in heaven, someday, but right now, here on earth. That result is so desirable and glorious, it is worth all the pain and heartache. That is why it can do nothing *but* rejoice! An authentic Christian is confident that the same Lord who permitted the pain to come will use it to bring about a highly desirable end. That is why we can be genuinely thankful—even in the midst of perplexity and sorrow.

There is an outstanding example of the unquenchable optimism of authentic Christianity in Acts 16. There, Paul and Silas find themselves at midnight in an inner dungeon in the city jail of Philippi. Their backs are raw and bloody from a terrible flogging received at the hands of the Roman authorities. Their feet are fastened in stocks. The future is uncertain and frightening. Anything could happen to them in the morning—even torture and death. There is no one around to be impressed by a show of courage, and no one to intervene and rescue them. Yet, despite all these reasons for pessimism and hopelessness, *Paul and Silas literally break into song!*

No one could accuse them of being phony or of putting up a good front just to keep up their spirits. They were genuinely thankful to God. They began to praise Him at midnight because they knew that, despite the apparent rebuff and lack of success, their objective had been accomplished. Now, the church they longed to plant in Philippi *could not be stopped!* That fact inspired them to break out in praise and thanksgiving. How could they have known what God had planned for them—an earthquake that would jar their chains loose, topple their prison walls, and set them free? They couldn't! They had no premonition at all of being set free. They were simply manifesting marks of authentic Christianity: unquenchable optimism and thanksgiving.

Mark No. 2: Unvarying success

The second mark of authentic Christianity is closely linked to the first. It is found in the next phrase in 2 Corinthians 2:14, "who always leads us in triumphal procession in Christ." Note how strongly Paul puts it: Jesus "*always* leads us" in triumph. Not occasionally. Not sometimes. *Always.* The apostle makes perfectly clear that the Christianity he has experienced presents a pattern of *unvarying success.* It never involves failure but invariably achieves its goals. It involves, as we have seen, struggles and hardships and tears. Sometimes, as on the cross at Calvary, the moment of triumph may even look like complete failure. But our triumph is always assured. Though the struggle may be desperate, it is never serious. It issues at last in the complete achievement of the objectives God has set for us. Even the opposition we encounter is made to serve the purposes of victory.

We must remember that these high-sounding words of Paul's are not mere evangelical pep talk. They were not uttered by a well-paid, highly respected pastor to a well-dressed suburban congregation in a modern American megachurch. These words were not given to thrill and entertain the Sunday morning audience, but to embolden and encourage those who were literally risking their lives and their families' lives every day for the cause of Christ. These words were written by a man who bore on his body the wounds of a servant of Jesus.

He had endured much difficulty, endless disappointments, and bitter persecution with great pain. Yet he could write with rugged truthfulness that Jesus *always* leads us in triumph.

This certainly does not mean that Paul's plans and goals were always realized, for they were not. He wanted to do many things that he was never able to accomplish. In Romans 9:3, Paul describes how he hungered to be used as a minister to Israel—"my brothers, those of my own race." He even expressed the willingness to be cut off from Christ if only the Israelites would be delivered. But he never achieved that objective. It is not his plans that are in view here, but God's. The triumph is Christ's, not Paul's.

The invariable mark of authentic Christianity is that, once we have discovered its radical secret, we can never fail. Our will, our dreams, our goals, our desires may be thwarted—but God's will and plan? Never! He can even weave our apparent failures into His overall design for ultimate triumph. In the life of an authentic Christian, every obstacle becomes an opportunity. Success is inevitable.

The liberty of prison

The unquenchable optimism of genuine Christianity shines through the first chapter of Paul's letter to his friends at Philippi. Writing as a prisoner in the city of Rome, confined to a private, rented home but chained day and night to a member of Caesar's imperial guard, Paul faces a very bleak future. He must soon appear before Nero Caesar to answer Jewish charges that could result in his death. He is no longer allowed to travel freely about the empire, preaching "the inexhaustible riches of Christ." He cannot even visit his beloved friends in the many churches he has founded.

What a time for discouragement! Yet no New Testament letter reflects greater confidence and rejoicing than Paul's letter to the Philippians. The reason for this confidence, Paul says, is twofold. He writes, "Now I want you to know, brothers, that what has happened to me has really served to advance the gospel" (Philippians 1:12). Then he lists two evidences to prove his point.

First, he says, "As a result, it has become clear throughout the whole palace guard and to everyone else that I am in chains for Christ" (Philippians 1:13). The palace guard (or, in some translations, the praetorian guard) is the imperial bodyguard. Since he is a prisoner of Caesar's, he must be guarded by Caesar's own hand-picked guard. The guard was largely made up of sons of noble families who were commissioned to spend a few years in Nero's palace guard. Later on, this select group would become the kingmakers of the empire, responsible for choosing succeeding emperors. They were impressive young men, the cream of the empire, in training for future positions of power and leadership.

Anyone who can read between the lines a bit will see what is happening here. It is clear that the Lord Jesus, in His role as King of the earth, has appointed Nero to be the chairman of the Committee for the Evangelization of the Roman Empire. Nero doesn't know this—but then emperors seldom know what is really going on in their empires. Remember that when the time came for the Son of God to be born in Bethlehem, his mother and her new husband were seventy miles away, living in Nazareth. So God commissioned Emperor Augustus to get Joseph and Mary down from Nazareth to Bethlehem. Augustus felt strangely moved to issue an imperial edict that everyone should go to his hometown to be taxed—and that did the trick!

In this case Nero has given orders that his imperial bodyguard should have charge of the apostle Paul. Every six hours, one of the future leaders of the Roman Empire was brought in, chained to Paul, and forcibly exposed to the life-changing gospel of Jesus Christ!

I suggest that if you want to feel sorry for anyone, don't feel sorry for Paul. Feel sorry for the young Roman bodyguard. Here he is, trying to live a quiet, pagan life and every so often he is ordered out and chained to this disturbing man who says the most amazing things about someone called Jesus of Nazareth, who has risen from the dead. As a result, one by one, these young men were being won to Christ. It is what you might call a chain reaction!

If you doubt that this was happening, just look at the next to the last verse of the Philippian letter: "All the saints send you greetings, especially those who belong to Caesar's household" (Philippians 4:22). Here is a band of young men, the political center of the empire, being infiltrated and conquered for Christ by an old man in chains who is awaiting trial for his life. It is not at all unlikely that some of the young men who accompanied Paul on his later journeys came from this very band.

This incident is a magnificent revelation of God's strategy—and, by contrast, of the weakness of human strategy. No human mind could have conceived this unique approach to the very heart of the empire. We humans are forever planning strategies for fulfilling the Great Commission, but what we come up with is usually banal, routine, unimaginative, and relatively ineffective. The noteworthy thing about God's strategy is that it is ingenious and totally unexpected.

Aided by opposition

The strategies of God are so powerful, compared with human plans and strategies, that He is able to take man's most vicious opposition and turn it to His own advantage. That is what is recorded in the early chapters of Acts. The church in Jerusalem was growing by leaps and bounds. Some 2,000 to 5,000 Christians were gathering together weekly and enjoying the tremendous fellowship and excitement. Yet it was all contained within the city walls. When God wanted to spread these good things among the nations, He permitted sharp opposition to arise. As a result, the early Christians were driven throughout the empire— all except the apostles.

I have learned to glimpse God's hand in these acts of opposition, and now read missionary reports from a different perspective. In recent years, I have seen many reports in missionary magazines saying in one way or another, "Terrible things are happening to our country. The doors are closing to the gospel. Opposition is rising. The government is trying to suppress all Christian witness. Our missionaries must soon pack up and get out." Without question, these missionaries and the national Christians in these countries are being oppressed and threatened, and they greatly need our prayers and support. Yet, when I read such reports, I have learned to say, "Thank God. At last the missionaries are being forced to relinquish control of the churches and the national church is taking over."

In Ethiopia, before World War II, the missionaries were driven out for twenty years, but when they came back in they found that the gospel had spread like wildfire, and there were far more Christians than if the missionaries had been allowed to stay. We have seen similar stories in other trouble spots around the world, notably China.

Paul makes a second point in his letter to the Philippians to support his claim that the things that happened to him had only served to advance the gospel. He says, *"Because of my chains,* most of the brothers in the Lord have been encouraged to speak the word of God more courageously and fearlessly" (Philippians 1:14, emphasis added). *Because Paul was a prisoner,* the Roman Christians were witnessing far more freely throughout the city than they would have done otherwise.

It was at this time that the first official Roman persecution against the Christians was beginning. Many, therefore, were afraid to speak of their faith. But then they saw that God—not Nero, not the Jewish leaders—was in complete charge of matters. With God in charge, they became emboldened to proclaim the gospel. As a result, there was far more effective outreach going on in Rome than if Paul had been free to preach at will. This fact has always suggested to me that perhaps the best way to evangelize a community would be to start by locking all the preachers up in jail! Other Christians might then begin to realize that they, too, have gifts for ministry, and would begin to exercise them in effective ways!

Living letters

Looking back on this incident with the benefit of twenty centuries of hindsight, we see a third proof of Paul's claim—a proof that even he could not have seen at the time. If we had been with Paul in that hired house in Rome and had asked him, "Paul, what do you think is the greatest work you have accomplished in your ministry through the power of Christ?" what would he have said? I feel sure his answer would have been, "The planting of churches in various cities." It was to these churches that his letters were written, and it was for them that he prayed daily. He called them "my joy and crown" and spent himself without restraint for them.

But now, looking back across the intervening centuries, we can see that the planting of these churches was not his greatest work after all. Every one of the churches he planted ceased its testimony long ago. In most cases, the very cities in which they existed lie in ruins today. The work of Paul that has persisted to this day has been the letters that he wrote when he was locked up and could do nothing else! Those letters have changed the world. They are among the most powerful documents known to men. No wonder Paul could write, "Thanks be to God, who always leads us in triumphal procession in Christ." It is an unmistakable mark of authentic Christianity.

Mark No. 3: Unforgettable impact

The third unmistakable mark follows immediately. After saying, "Thanks be to God, who always leads us in triumphal procession in Christ," Paul continues with this beautiful statement of the impact we have as authentic Christians: "and through us spreads everywhere *the fragrance of the knowledge of him*" (2 Corinthians 2:14, emphasis added). God tells us that our lives should be spent giving off a fragrance, a perfume, a pleasing bouquet—not only to other people, but to God. Enlarging on this thought, Paul adds: "For we are to God the aroma of Christ among those who are being saved and those who are perishing. To the one we are the smell of death; to the other, the fragrance of life. And who is equal to such a task?" (2 Corinthians 2:15–16).

Most men have had the experience of being in a room when a strikingly beautiful woman enters. Before she came in, she applied a touch here and there of

White Diamonds, and as she passes through the room, she leaves behind a lingering fragrance. Consciously or unconsciously, all the males in the room are affected by that fragrance. Weeks or months later, they may catch a wisp of that fragrance again—and immediately, the image of that beautiful woman flashes into their minds. The fragrance has made her unforgettable.

That is the picture Paul gives here. Authentic Christianity leaves an *unforgettable impression* on those who encounter it. Christians are responsible for the enduring impact they make. As Paul suggests, the impact may be in one of two directions. Christians either increase opposition to Christ (death to death) or they lead toward faith and life (life to life). If your life is one that reflects radical, authentic Christianity, people become either bitter or better through contact with you. But one thing cannot happen: people will never remain the same. Those who are determined to die are pushed on toward death by coming into contact with authentic Christianity. Those who are seeking to live are helped on into life. Jesus certainly had this quality about Him. No one ever came into contact with Him and went away the same.

Many commentators on this passage conclude that Paul had in mind here a typical Roman triumph. When a Roman general returned to the capital after a successful campaign, he was granted a triumph by the senate. A great procession passed through the streets of Rome displaying the captives which were taken in the course of the conquest. Some people went before the chariot of the conqueror, bearing garlands of flowers and pots of fragrant incense. They were the prisoners who were destined to live and return to their captured country to govern it under Roman rule. Other prisoners followed behind the chariot dragging chains and heavy manacles. These were doomed to execution, for the Romans felt they could not trust them. As the procession went on through the cheering crowds, the incense pots and fragrant flowers were to the first group a fragrance from life unto life while the same aroma was to the second group a fragrance of death to death.

This is the effect of the gospel as it touches the world through the life of an authentic Christian. Authentic Christianity leaves a lingering fragrance to God of Jesus Christ, no matter what—but to human beings, it is either a fragrance of death to death or of life to life.

But what about phony Christianity? That's another matter altogether—it's just a bad smell! You've certainly heard the old one-liner—"Old fishermen never die— they only smell that way." The same can be said for false Christianity: it never dies; it only smells that way.

Mark No. 4: Unimpeachable integrity

The fourth mark of genuine Christianity is found in 2 Corinthians 2:17: "Unlike so many, we do not peddle the word of God for profit. On the contrary, in Christ we speak before God with sincerity, like men sent from God." Remember, that is not a description of Christian pastors but of all Christians. It has great application to pastors and others in the ministry, but its primary reference is to common, ordinary Christians who have learned the secret of authentic Christianity.

Christians can be described in two ways, negatively and positively. Negatively, they are not peddlers. The word means a huckster, a street salesman. Occasionally I hear Christian witnessing described as "selling the gospel." I cringe when I hear that because I don't believe Christians are meant to be salespeople for God. The idea here is that of a street hawker who has certain wares that he considers attractive and that he peddles on the corner as people are passing by. He makes his living by peddling his wares.

Much Christian preaching and witnessing can be described that way. People select certain attractive features from the Scriptures and use these as "selling points." Healing is a case in point. It is a legitimate subject for study and practice, but when singled out and harped on continually, especially when a pitch for large, sacrificial offerings is linked to it, healing can quickly lead to hucksterism. Prophecy can serve the same purpose. I am troubled by anyone who is known only as a prophetic teacher, for that person has picked out something that is attractive (and even sensational) from the Word. If that is all he ever teaches, he is not declaring the whole counsel of God. He is a peddler, making a living by hawking certain wares from the Scriptures. Paul says authentic Christianity does not hawk its truth like a peddler selling goods in the street.

Four qualities of integrity

Our integrity as authentic Christians is characterized by four qualities, according to this passage. First quality: we speak "with sincerity." In other words, we are to be honest people. We must mean what we say. The world admires sincerity and feels it is the ultimate expression of character—but according to Paul, sincerity is just the beginning of character, God's minimum expectation of authentic Christians. The very least we should expect from ourselves as Christians is that we thoroughly believe and practice what we say.

Second quality: Paul says we are "sent from God" (or, as the Revised Standard Version renders it, "commissioned by God"). This speaks of our *purpose* as authentic Christians. We are not to be idle dreamers with no definite objective in view. We have been commissioned as military officers are commissioned. We have been given a definite task and specific assignments that constitute our purpose in life and in ministry. We are purposeful people with an end in view, an object to attain, a goal to accomplish, and we do not merely preach or witness as though that were a goal in itself.

Third quality: Paul says we do all this "before God" (or, in the RSV, "in the sight of God"). This indicates an attitude of transparency, of openness to investigation. To walk in the sight of other people permits us to hide our sins and contradictions behind a facade. But to walk in the sight of God requires total honesty with Him and with ourselves, because nothing can be hidden from God's sight. This does not mean we can live sinlessly, but rather that there must be no cover-up or evasion of the facts of our sin when it occurs. It means there are no areas of denial. All is evaluated and tested by the purity and knowledge and wisdom of God—and what is sinful, we confess and we repent of before God. A man who walks in the sight of God is more interested in his inner reality than his outer reputation. He can be completely trusted. You can even believe his golf score and the size of the trout he caught. If you can teach your young people to live in the sight of God, you will even be able to trust them in the back seat of a car.

Fourth and final quality: we speak "in Christ." What quality does that indicate? *Authority!* Paul states it clearly in 2 Corinthians 5:20—"We are therefore Christ's ambassadors, as though God were making his appeal through us." Ambassadors are authorized spokesmen. They have power to act and make covenants on behalf of others. Authentic Christians are not powerless servants. We speak words and deliver messages that heaven honors.

All of these qualities add up to *unimpeachable integrity*. People of sincerity, purpose, transparency, and authority are utterly trustworthy. You can ring a gold coin on their conscience. Their word is their bond, and they can be counted on to come through. They are responsible and faithful individuals. That is the fourth great mark of real Christianity.

At this point in the Scripture text, we come to a chapter division. This is unfortunate, because it divides two chapters that belong together. The apostle has not finished his line of reasoning, so it's best to ignore the division and read right on, to find the fifth mark of authentic Christianity: "Are we beginning to commend ourselves again? Or do we need, like some people, letters of recommendation to you or from you?" (2 Corinthians 3:1).

Mark No. 5: Undeniable reality

Paul is aware that he is beginning to sound arrogant. He knows there are some in Corinth who will immediately take these words in that way. Indeed, it is obvious from his words that some had even suggested in previous correspondence that the next time he came to Corinth he bring letters of recommendation from some of the Twelve in Jerusalem! They were thinking of Paul as though he were a man entirely like themselves: so continually praising himself that no one would believe him without confirmation from more objective sources. But Paul says to them, "You yourselves are our letter, written on our hearts, known and read by everybody. You show that you are a letter from Christ, the result of our ministry, written not with ink but with the Spirit of the living God, not on tablets of stone but on tablets of human hearts" (2 Corinthians 3:2–3).

He is saying, in effect, "You want letters of recommendation to prove I have authority as a messenger of

God? Why, you yourselves are all the recommendation I need! Look what has happened to you. Are you any different since you came to Christ through my word? Your own hearts will bear witness to yourselves and before the world that the message you heard from us and which has changed your lives is from God." In 1 Corinthians 6, Paul made reference to "the sexually immoral . . . idolaters . . . adulterers . . . male prostitutes . . . homosexual offenders . . . thieves . . . greedy . . . drunkards . . . slanderers . . . [and] swindlers" he had found in Corinth. "And that is what some of you were," he added (verses 9–11). But now they had been washed, sanctified, and justified by the name of the Lord Jesus Christ. These changes validated Paul's message.

The Corinthians had written to Paul about their newfound joy and the hope and meaning that had been brought into their lives. They described to him their deliverance from shame and guilt, their freedom from fear and hostility, from darkness and death. So he says to them, in effect, "This is your confirmation. You yourselves are walking letters from God, known and read by all men, written by the Spirit of God in your hearts." Here is the final mark of genuine Christianity: *undeniable reality,* a change that cannot be explained on any other terms than God at work. Paul did not need letters of recommendation when this kind of change was evident in the lives of his hearers.

I once heard of a Christian who had been an alcoholic for years and then was converted. Someone asked him, "Now that you are a Christian, do you believe the miracles of the New Testament?" He answered, "Yes, I do." The other man said, "Do you believe that story about Jesus changing water into wine?" He said, "I sure do." The other said, "How can you believe such nonsense?" The Christian replied, "I'll tell you how;

because in our house Jesus changed whiskey into furniture!" That is the mark of authenticity. Such a marked change occurs only under the impulse of a powerful relationship that substitutes the love of Christ for the love of drink.

These are the five unmistakable signs of genuine Christianity: unquenchable optimism, unvarying success, unforgettable impact, unimpeachable integrity, and undeniable reality. They are always present whenever the real thing is being manifested. Mere religion tries to imitate these marks, but is never quite able to pull it off. By comparison with these marks, phony Christianity is always exposed as a shabby, shoddy imitation that quickly folds when the real pressure is on. The remarkable thing is not that men seek to imitate these genuine graces, for we all have been hypocrites of one kind or another since our birth. The truly remarkable thing is that becoming a Christian does not of itself guarantee that these Christian graces will be manifest in us. It is not *being* a Christian that produces these, but *living* as a Christian. There is a knowledge we must have and a choice we must make before these virtues will be consistently present. The secret awaits us in the next chapter.

The Secret

Turn on the radio or TV, and within minutes you'll be bombarded with messages called "advertising." Each of these advertising messages has a different look, a distinct sound, but all of them promise essentially the same thing: the secret of fulfillment, satisfaction, success, happiness. "Drink Dipsy-Cola and really live!" "Do your friends ignore you? Try Charm deodorant, the underarm security!" "Read How To Be A Phenomenon, the amazing new success story." "Sign up for our six-week course, 'The Power Ploy'—it will change your life!" "Find the romance you've always wanted, sail on the S.S. Slopover to the Islands of Mystery."

These messages used to inflict themselves on you for periods of only thirty to sixty seconds at a time. Now, however, if you are an insomniac with cable TV, you can watch thirty-minute "infomercials" that will prove to you that the secret to happiness can be found on an exercise machine, or through owning your own vending machine route, or by dialing up a psychic hotline. Let's face it: Whether the message lasts for half a minute or half an hour, it's all a lie. You won't find the secret by purchasing a product at the department store, cruising aboard the good ship *Slopover*, or calling that number at the bottom of your TV screen.

But don't despair! The secret can be found. It truly is available to you. Paul talks about it in 2 Corinthians 2—and we're going to reveal it right here and now! (Sorry, no credit cards accepted, and no C.O.D.s—the secret the apostle is talking about is not for sale at any price. It is absolutely free!)

The source of our sufficiency

Remember the five marks of authentic Christianity we examined in the previous chapter: unquenchable optimism, unvarying success, unforgettable impact, unimpeachable integrity, and undeniable reality. These five marks came into focus for us as we read Paul's description of his own experience and ministry in 2 Corinthians 2. Yet Paul also raised an important question in that chapter—a question I deliberately bypassed in order to save it for this chapter. After listing those five marks of an authentic Christian, Paul asks the reader, "And who is equal to such a task?"

Now, let's take that question very seriously. Try to answer it! Who, indeed, is equal to such a task? Who among us demonstrates the kind of unquenchable optimism, unvarying success, unforgettable impact, unimpeachable integrity, and undeniable reality that is supposed to mark the life of an authentic Christian? Who is a consistent model of these qualities? Am I? Are you?

Are you equal to the task of continually, unfailingly, consistently manifesting a cheerful, confident spirit? An ability always to come out on top? A powerful, positive influence on others? Complete trustworthiness? And such a reliable, realistic demonstration of these qualities that no one is ever in doubt about them? What self-help course can we take to learn how to live like this? What product can we buy, what book can we read to find the secret? Who is equal to such a task?

The question hangs in the air, waiting for an answer. Immediately a half dozen or so possibilities come to mind, for the question is so important that half the world's activity is devoted to finding an answer. Paul, however, does not leave us groping for an answer to his searching question. In 2 Corinthians 3:4–6 he gives us his forthright answer:

> Such confidence as this is ours through Christ before God. Not that we are competent to claim anything for ourselves, but our competence comes from God. He has made us competent as ministers of a new covenant—not of the letter but of the Spirit; for the letter kills, but the Spirit gives life.

He puts the great secret before us in unmistakable terms: "This confidence is ours through Christ! Our sufficiency is from God!" Lest anyone miss the implications of that, he puts the same truth negatively: "Not that we are competent or sufficient in ourselves! No, our sufficiency comes from God alone." Nothing coming from us; everything coming from God! That is the secret of secrets—the secret of true fulfillment, satisfaction, and success.

Live it—don't waste it

To live in this way, drawing our sufficiency from God, is what it means to be "competent as ministers of a new covenant." He sharply contrasts this way of life with the old covenant, the dead written code, the "letter" that "kills." To live with nothing coming from us and everything coming from God is to live in the Spirit. The Spirit continually gives Life with a capital *L*. This is the secret that produced the confident spirit that characterized Paul and empowered him to spread the fragrance of the knowledge of Christ everywhere he went. The language he uses reminds us immediately of the words of Jesus to His disciples: "I am the vine; you are the branches. . . . apart from me you can do nothing" (John 15:5). Neither Jesus nor Paul means to imply that no human activity is possible without reliance upon God. Both the world and the church are full of examples to the contrary.

But both Jesus and Paul teach that activity dependent upon human resources for its success will, in the end, accomplish nothing. It will have no permanent value. Men may praise it and emulate it, but God will count it for what it is—wasted effort. Just such a life is described in the plaintive question of T. S. Eliot:

All our knowledge brings us nearer to our ignorance,
All our ignorance brings us nearer to death,
But nearness to death no nearer to God.
Where is the life we have lost in living?
—from "The Rock"

Where, indeed? We are forced to honestly admit that we deliberately waste a good deal of our life in useless dreaming and profitless activity. But not all of it! At times we give it the old college try, sometimes we are earnest and serious and do our level best to act as we ought and do what we should. The results often appear very impressive to us, and even to others, but when we think of our approaching death, it all seems rather vain and futile. That's when we ask, "Where is the life we have lost in living?"

The apostle indicates that the secret of an effective, meaningful life lies in what he calls "the new covenant." Jesus referred to this "new covenant" when He passed the cup to His disciples at the institution of the Lord's Supper: "This cup is the new covenant in my blood, which is poured out for you" (Luke 22:20). This cup, taken with the bread, is to remind us of the central truth of our lives: Jesus died *for* us in order that He may live *in* us. His life in us is the power by which we live a true Christian life. That is the new covenant.

It is important to understand the meaning of the word *covenant*. There are, according to Paul, two covenants at work in human life. One is the new covenant, which Paul would describe as "nothing coming from me, everything from God." This is in direct contrast to the old covenant, which could be described as "everything coming from me and nothing coming from God." The root idea of covenant, both in Paul's day and ours, is that of an agreement essential to all further relationship.

If two men go into business together, they form a partnership. The terms of their relationship are carefully spelled out so they will have a framework within which to work. Marriage is also a type of covenant in which a man and a woman agree to share all they have and to stick together against all obstacles till death. Nations sign treaties with one another to determine the conditions under which they will work together. All these examples are forms of covenants, and it is apparent from these that a covenant is fundamental and essential to all human endeavor.

But the most fundamental covenant of all is the one that forms the basis of human life itself. We may not often think of it in this way, but no activity is possible to us that does not rest upon an underlying covenant. We could not talk, sing, walk, speak, pray, run, think, or breathe without that covenant. It is an arrangement made by God with the human race, whereby we are furnished the life and energy we need to perform what God wants us to do. We do not provide our own energy. We are dependent creatures, needing a constant supply from God the Creator in order to live and breathe.

Now the great thing that Paul declares to us in this passage—confirmed in both the Old and the New Testaments—is that this fundamental arrangement for living comes to us in one of two ways. There is an "old" way which, as we shall see in the next chapter, is linked inextricably with the Old Testament law of Moses—the written code, the "letter" which kills.

But through Jesus Christ, there is a "new" way that results in life that is unquenchably optimistic, characterized by unfeigned success, makes unforgettable impact, operates with unimpeachable integrity, and confronts the world with a testimony of undeniable reality. Having discovered the implications of this new covenant, the apostle finds himself qualified to live as God intended him to live, and it is through discovering these same implications for ourselves that we shall find ourselves qualified by God to live as God intends us to live today.

How Paul found the secret

Since the apostle uses his own experience as the example of the kind of life he has in view, it will be helpful to trace the way and the time that he came to learn this transforming truth for himself. If you think it all came to him in that one dramatic moment in the dust of the Damascus road when he discovered the true identity of Jesus Christ and yielded himself to his lordly claims, then you are far from the truth. It is true that Paul was born again at that moment; it is true that he understood for the first time that Jesus was indeed the Son of God; it is true that the center of this ardent young Pharisee's life was forever changed from living for his own advancement to desiring the eternal glory of Jesus Christ. But it may be of great encouragement to many of us who struggle in the Christian life to learn that Paul also went through a period of probably ten years after his conversion before he began to live in the fullness of the new covenant. And it was during this time that, from God's point of view, he was an abject failure in living the Christian life!

We can piece together from Acts 9 and several other Scriptures the full account of Paul's conversion experience and what happened to produce the tremendous change in his life. Here is a description of what took place after the experience of the Damascus road:

> Saul [Paul] spent several days with the disciples in Damascus. At once he began to preach in the synagogues that Jesus is the Son of God. All those who heard him were astonished and asked, "Isn't he the man who raised havoc in Jerusalem among those who call on this name? And hasn't he come here to take them as prisoners to the chief priests?" (Acts 9:19–21).

It is clear from these words that it all happened within a very few days after Paul's conversion and his baptism at the hands of Ananias. Paul began immediately, with characteristic vigor, to *proclaim* (herald, announce) the deity of Jesus ("He is the Son of

God"). This truth he had learned in the glory of the light that flamed about him on the road to Damascus. Then Luke, without giving any indication in the text whatever, goes on in his account to something that did not take place for at least several months after the above events and which may not have occurred for as long as three years afterward: "Yet Saul grew more and more powerful and baffled the Jews living in Damascus by proving that Jesus is the Christ" (Acts 9:22).

Note that Paul's (or Saul's) message is here said to be in the form of "proving" that Jesus is the Christ. There is a great difference between *proclaiming* Jesus as the Son of God and *proving* that He is the Christ. Luke only hints at what made the difference in his phrase, "Saul grew more and more powerful," but Paul himself tells us in more detail what happened in his life. We find his description of that time in his letter to the Galatians.

From proclaiming to proving

Many scholars consider the Galatian letter to be the earliest of Paul's epistles. Whether it is or not is uncertain, but it is clear that in it Paul defends his apostleship and describes what happened to him after his conversion. He writes:

> When God, who set me apart from birth and called me by his grace, was pleased to reveal his Son in me so that I might preach him among the Gentiles, I did not consult any man, nor did I go up to Jerusalem to see those who were apostles before I was, but I went immediately into Arabia and later returned to Damascus (Galatians 1:15–17).

We learn from this account that what served to greatly strengthen young Saul at this time was that he went away into Arabia and then returned to Damascus. What did he do in Arabia? Scripture doesn't tells us, but I don't think it is difficult to figure out. We need only imagine the shock to this young man's life that his conversion produced to realize that he desperately needed time to go back through the Old Testament Scriptures and learn how his discovery of the truth about Jesus of Nazareth related to the revelation of the prophets which he had trusted ever since he was a child.

As a Pharisee and based on what he knew of the Scriptures, he had been convinced that Jesus of Nazareth was a fraud. Now he knew better—yet somehow, somewhere, he must work out the mental confusion this new discovery produced in him. Arabia supplied the opportunity. So into Arabia he went, the scrolls of the Old Testament tucked under his arm. As we might well surmise, he found Jesus on every page. How the old, familiar passages must have glowed with new light as, beginning with Moses and all the prophets, the Spirit of God interpreted to him the things that belonged to Jesus. It was no wonder that when he returned to Damascus he came "greatly strengthened." And no wonder, too, that Paul went into the same synagogues, armed with his newfound knowledge, and began proclaiming for the first time Jesus is the Son of God. In the Jewish houses of worship, he turned from passage to passage of the Jewish Scriptures and "proved" (Greek: "to knit together") that Jesus was the Christ, the Messiah foretold by the Old Testament.

A basket case

Then things took a turn for the worse. To young Saul's chagrin the Jews of Damascus were not at all responsive to his powerful arguments. Luke tells us what happened:

After many days had gone by, the Jews conspired to kill him, but Saul learned of their plan. Day and night they kept close watch on the city gates in order to kill him. But his followers took him by night and lowered him in a basket through an opening in the wall (Acts 9:23–25).

What a burning humiliation to this dedicated young Christian! Paul had become—quite literally—a basket case! How confused and puzzled he must have been as all his dreams of conquest in the name of Jesus were brought to this sudden and degrading halt. How humiliating to be let down over the wall in a basket like a common criminal escaping from the reach of the law! How shameful, how discouraging! Once over the wall, he slips off into the darkness of the night, bewildered, humiliated, and thoroughly discouraged. He stated later that it was both the lowest point in his life and the beginning of the greatest discovery he ever made.

Where does he go from there? Luke tells us immediately, "When he came to Jerusalem, he tried to join the disciples, but they were all afraid of him, not believing that he really was a disciple" (Acts 9:26). Paul's own account agrees with this exactly. In Galatians 1:18–19 he says, "Then after three years, I went up to Jerusalem to get acquainted with Peter and stayed with him fifteen days. I saw none of the other apostles—only James, the Lord's brother." How he managed to break through the fear barrier to see these two men is given us by Luke:

Barnabas took him and brought him to the apostles. He told them how Saul on his journey had seen the Lord and that the Lord had spoken to him, and how in Damascus he had preached fearlessly in the name of Jesus. So Saul stayed with them and moved about freely in Jerusalem, speaking boldly in the name of the Lord. He talked and debated with the Grecian Jews, but they tried to kill him (Acts 9:27–29).

It is a familiar pattern. Once again the ardent young Christian is determined to persuade the Greek-speaking Jews that Jesus is the promised Messiah of the Old Testament. Once again a plot against his life is set in motion. It is the Damascus story all over again.

Get out!
But at this point there occurs another of those gaps in Luke's account that we must fill in from Paul's own account elsewhere. Luke does not relate to us young Saul's reaction to the opposition he received when he preached to the Jerusalem Jews. But knowing his ambitious and dedicated heart, it must have been one of severe discouragement. At any rate, years later, he mentioned this event in his great defense to the Jerusalem mob when he was arrested in the temple precincts and saved from certain death only by the timely intervention of the Romans. In Acts 22 he tells us, "When I returned to Jerusalem and was praying at the temple, I fell into a trance and saw the Lord speaking. 'Quick!' he said to me. 'Leave Jerusalem immediately, because they will not accept your testimony about me'" (Acts 22:17–18).

It is surely understandable that young Saul would seek the comfort of the temple at this discouraging moment. Again his efforts to bear a convincing witness for Christ had failed, once again men were seeking to find an opportunity to kill him, and he had no positive results with which to encourage himself. No wonder he went into the temple to pray. And there, to this discouraged disciple, the Lord Jesus appeared—yet His message was anything but encouraging. "Get out of Jerusalem," said Jesus. "They will not receive your testimony concerning me." At this point Saul began to argue with Jesus: " 'Lord,' I replied, 'these men know that I went from one synagogue to another to imprison and beat those who believe in you. And when the blood of your martyr Stephen was shed, I stood there giving my approval and guarding the clothes of those who were killing him'" (Acts 22:19–20).

In these words Saul gave himself away. We can now see what he was depending on for success in his witnessing efforts. It is apparent that he saw himself as the one person who was eminently qualified to reach the Jews for Christ. His argument says in effect, "Lord, you don't understand this situation. If you send me out of Jerusalem you are going to miss the opportunity of a lifetime. If anyone understands how these Jews think and reason, it is me. I was one of them. I speak their language. I know how they react. I understand their background. I too am an Israelite, a Hebrew of the Hebrews, circumcised on the eighth day, of the tribe of Benjamin. I was a Pharisee like they are. I walked before the law blameless. I even persecuted the church, as they are now doing. Why, when the martyr Stephen was killed, I even kept the garments of those who murdered him! Lord, don't send me away. I have what it takes to reach these men. Don't miss this opportunity!"

Jesus' answer is abrupt and to the point. Paul tells us himself, "Then the Lord said to me, 'Go; I will send you far away to the Gentiles'" (Acts 22:21). What a shattering blow! How crushed young Saul must have been! But to indicate how the church agreed with the Lord at this point, Luke tells us, "When the brothers learned of this [the plot to kill Saul], they took him down to Caesarea and sent him off to Tarsus" (Acts 9:30).

Tarsus was Paul's hometown. There is no tougher place to go as a Christian than back home. Paul had tried his best to serve his newfound Lord with all the ability and energy he could muster. But it amounted to exactly nothing. In fact, at this point, Luke records a rather astonishing thing after Paul's exile to Tarsus: "Then the church throughout Judea, Galilee and Samaria enjoyed a time of peace. It was strengthened; and encouraged by the Holy Spirit, it grew in numbers, living in the fear of the Lord" (Acts 9:31).

The record shows that at first the apostle Paul was not so much the dynamic history-changing missionary he later became. No, initially the apostle Paul was really something of a "consecrated blunderer"! In his earnest, fervent, good-hearted way, he went about, preaching the gospel, and stirring up all kinds of anger and hostility among the Jews! When this "dedicated disputer" was eliminated—sent away to his hometown of Tarsus—the church finally had peace! It began to grow! Isn't that amazing?

Saul goes off to Tarsus to nurse his wounds, his ego shattered and his plans dissolved in despair. For ten years he is not heard of again—not until an awakening breaks out in Antioch of Syria and the church in Jerusalem sends Barnabas down to investigate. When Barnabas finds "a great number of people [are being] brought to the Lord" (Acts 11:24), he knows help is needed.

In verses 25–26, we read, "Then Barnabas went to Tarsus to look for Saul, and when he found him, he brought him to Antioch. So for a whole year Barnabas and Saul met with the church and taught great numbers of people. The disciples were called Christians first at Antioch." It was a different Saul who came to Antioch with Barnabas. Chastened, humbled, taught by the Spirit, he began to teach the Word of God, and from there launched into the great missionary thrust that would take him eventually to the limits of the Roman Empire and spread the gospel with explosive force throughout the world.

Are you a basket case?

What made the difference? Writing to the Corinthians many years later Paul makes one brief reference to the event that triggered a line of teaching that would culminate in a clear understanding and acceptance of what he came to call "the new covenant." The Corinthian church had written to Paul and brazenly suggested to him that he would be more effective if he would boast once in awhile in his accomplishments. To this the apostle replied in his second letter, chapter 11: " If I must boast, I will boast of the things that show my weakness. The God and Father of the Lord Jesus, who is to be praised forever, knows that I am not lying" (2 Corinthians 11:30–31).

What he is going to say will be such a shock to them that he takes a solemn vow that he is telling them the truth, otherwise they may think he is joking or playing with them. Then he tells them what his boast is: " In Damascus the governor under King Aretas had the city of the Damascenes guarded in order to arrest me. But I was lowered in a basket from a window in the wall and slipped through his hands" (2 Corinthians 11:32–33).

"That," says Paul, "is my boast. That is the greatest event of my life since my conversion. When I became a basket case, then I began to learn the truth that has changed my life and explains my power." What was that life-changing truth? Let Paul put it in his own words, from his letter to the Philippians:

> If anyone else thinks he has reasons to put confidence in the flesh, I have more: circumcised

on the eighth day, of the people of Israel, of the tribe of Benjamin, a Hebrew of Hebrews; in regard to the law, a Pharisee; as for zeal, persecuting the church; as for legalistic righteousness, faultless. But whatever was to my profit I now consider loss for the sake of Christ. What is more, I consider everything a loss compared to the surpassing greatness of knowing Christ Jesus my Lord, for whose sake I have lost all things. I consider them rubbish, that I may gain Christ" (Philippians 3:4–8).

The word he uses for "consider them rubbish" refers to common, barnyard dung. What he once regarded as qualifying him to be a success before God and men (his ancestry, his orthodoxy, his morality, and his activity) he now regards as so much manure compared to depending upon the working of Jesus Christ within him. He has learned how to shift from the old covenant (everything coming from me, nothing coming from God) to the new covenant (nothing coming from me, everything coming from God), which gives life. He is no longer highly qualified to be utterly useless but is able to say: "My sufficiency is from God, who has qualified me to be a minister of a new covenant."

Have you become a basket case yet? Have you reached that place which Jesus described as "blessed"? "Blessed are the poor in spirit, for theirs is the kingdom of heaven." To be "poor in spirit" is to be utterly bankrupt before some demand of life, and then discover it to be a blessing because it forced you to depend wholly upon the Lord at work in you. That is where you learn the truth of the new covenant, and nowhere else. We have much to learn yet about *why* it works, but you can find out *how* it works only when you experience it yourself.

Two Splendors

G OD LOVES VISUAL AIDS. He has scattered them all over the earth and hung them in the sky. Jesus made rich use of God's visual examples to help His hearers including you and me—to understand spiritual truth:

- "See how the lilies of the field grow."
- "It is easier for a camel to go through the eye of a needle than for a rich man to enter the kingdom of God."
- "Do not throw your pearls to pigs. If you do, they may trample them under their feet, and then turn and tear you to pieces."
- "You are the salt of the earth."
- "I am the vine; you are the branches."

I suspect that the whole world of nature may have been created to illustrate, on a physical and visible level, what is going on all the time in the invisible, spiritual realm. Elizabeth Barrett Browning put it exactly,

Earth's crammed with heaven;
And every common bush aflame with God.
But only those who see take off their shoes,
The rest sit round it—and pluck blackberries!
—from "Aurora Leigh"

Two faces of glory

To help the Corinthians (and us) understand what he meant by "the old covenant" and "the new covenant" the apostle Paul used two very helpful visual aids. They are borrowed from the story of the giving of the law from Mt. Sinai and the subsequent conduct of Moses with the people of Israel. He first calls attention to the glory of Moses' face:

> Now if the ministry that brought death, which was engraved in letters on stone, came with glory, so that the Israelites could not look steadily at the face of Moses because of its glory, fading though it was, will not the ministry of the Spirit be even more glorious? (2 Corinthians 3:7–8).

The old covenant, which Paul calls "a ministry that brought death"(2 Corinthians 3:7), was aptly symbolized by the shining of Moses' face when he came down from the mountain with the law "engraved in letters on stone." There was a certain glory or splendor about the law. It attracted people and awakened their admiration and interest. That's what glory always does; it is captivating and attractive. To this day the law retains that attractiveness. All over the world the Ten Commandments are held in high regard, even by those who regularly break them (which includes us all). Men pay lip service to them as the ideal of life, even though they may say they are impractical and impossible to keep. Everywhere men dream of achieving a dedication that will enable them to fulfill these glorious ideals.

But Paul emphasizes the even greater splendor of the new covenant. It is far more attractive and exciting than the law. Reliance on the old covenant cannot compare with life in the new. And just as the glory of the old covenant has its symbol (the shining face of Moses), so the new covenant has its symbol as well. Paul mentions it a little further on in the passage and obviously intended it to be set in contrast with the face of Moses. He says, "God, who said, 'Let light shine out of darkness,' made his light shine in our hearts to give us the light of the knowledge of the glory of God in the face of Christ" (2 Corinthians 4:6).

Here, then, are the two splendors—the face of Moses and the face of Jesus Christ. Both are exciting; one much more than the other. They stand for the two covenants, or arrangements, by which human life is lived. Both have power to attract men, but one is a fading glory and the other is eternal. The unredeemed world lives continually by looking at the face of Moses. The Christian can live by either, but never both at the same time. It is always one or the other at any given moment of a Christian's life. "No one can serve two masters," said Jesus. "Either he will hate the one and love the other, or he will be devoted to the one and despise the other" (Matthew 6:24). So in the true Christian's life, the activity of each moment derives its value from whether he is, at that moment, symbolically looking at the face of Moses or at the face of Jesus Christ.

The trouble with law

At this point we must seek to understand more clearly something of great importance. Someone may well raise the question, "Why does Paul link the old covenant with the law and call it a "ministry that brought death" when in Romans 7 he says that the law is "holy, righteous, and good"? How could the shining face of Moses—which came as a result of spending forty days alone with God—be a symbol of something that kills? As a matter of fact, Paul himself raises the same question in his discussion of the law in Romans 7 when he says, "What shall we say, then? Is the law sin?" His forceful response is, "Certainly not!" (Romans 7:7). And after showing that it was by means of the law that he found out the extent of his sin, he adds, "So then, the law is holy, and the commandment is holy, righteous and good" (Romans 7:12).

In Romans 8:3 the apostle gives us the clue that explains this enigma: "What the law was powerless to do *in that it was weakened by the sinful nature,* God did by sending his own Son in the likeness of sinful man to be a sin offering" (emphasis added). The problem, therefore, is not the law; it is what the law must work with, that is, the flesh. The word *flesh* does not refer here to the meat and bones that make up the body, but is an equivalent term for fallen human nature—human nature acting apart from Christ. The law, in any of its forms, was needed and was given only because the flesh exists. The law is unnecessary except for the flesh. Paul said to Timothy,

We know that the law is good if one uses it properly. We also know that law is made not for the righteous but for lawbreakers and rebels, the ungodly and sinful, the unholy and irreligious; for those who kill their fathers or mothers, for murderers, for adulterers and perverts, for slave traders and liars and perjurers—and for whatever else is contrary to the sound doctrine that conforms to the glorious gospel of the blessed God, which he entrusted to me (1 Timothy 1:8–11).

A walking civil war

These verses should not be read as though Paul were referring only to pagans, heathens, criminals, and perverts. Christians, even the best and saintliest of them, are sometimes "lawbreakers" and "rebels," guilty of ungodliness and sin, adulterous and perverted (in their thoughts if not their actions), and all too frequently "liars" or "perjurers." Certainly, many "Christian sins" are caught up in the phrase, "whatever else is contrary to the sound doctrine." Certainly the sin nature is at work in Christians, and whenever it is, the law is required. The law is made for our humanity, our sin nature, and is unnecessary apart from it. Human beings require the law, for "through the law we became conscious of sin."

Since this is so clearly true, it helps us to see that the essential conflict between the old covenant (the face of Moses) and the new covenant (the face of Jesus Christ) is, in reality, the struggle between the flesh and the Spirit. Each of us is, in effect, a walking civil war. The flesh wars against the Spirit within us, just as Paul observed in his letter to the Galatians: "The sinful nature desires what is contrary to the Spirit, and the Spirit what is contrary to the sinful nature. They are in conflict with each other, so that you do not do what you want" (Galatians 5:17). It is because of this inevitable tie between the flesh and the law that Paul, in 2 Corinthians, refers to the law as a "ministry that brought death" and says that "the letter kills." In reality, it is the flesh that produces death, but the law, though holy, just, and good, cannot be separated from it.

The preceding arguments may seem a bit ponderous, but I urge you to think them through carefully, for perhaps nothing has contributed more to the present weakness of the church than a failure to understand the nature and character of the flesh. It may greatly help us to see this clearly if we go back to the beginning and learn how the flesh came into existence and what its essence is.

When Adam came from the hand of God, he was a perfect man, as God intended man to be. He was, therefore, acting by the power of God. Everything he did was accomplished by the indwelling Spirit of power. We know this from the analogy to Jesus who was the second Adam. Jesus tells us repeatedly that whatever He did or said was not done out of any energy or might of His own, but as He plainly put it, "the Father, living in me, who is doing his work" (John 14:10). He was living by the new covenant, "everything coming from God, nothing coming from me." In fact, he said, "The Son can do nothing by himself" (John 5:19).

That is how Adam lived before the fall. When he tended the garden, he did so by the energy and power of God. When he named the animals, he named them by the wisdom and power of God. Adam brought to each task the fullness of divine resources, available to whatever degree was required by the task itself. This is, of course, what man was and is intended to be, the bearer and dwelling place of God. Adam was the "house" of God, and all that he did was a manifestation of God's power.

The choice of activity was left up to Adam. That was his part. He was the chooser; God himself was the doer. Adam could do anything he wanted, go any place within the garden he chose, eat anything he liked—except one thing. God planted a tree in the garden, and placed it beyond Adam's *right* to choose—but not beyond his *power* to choose. It was the tree of the knowledge of good and evil. One day, in conspiracy with his wife, Adam made that fatal choice.

Since everyone who has ever lived since Adam was made in the image of fallen Adam, we can understand something of what happened when Adam ate the forbidden fruit. The Spirit of God was immediately removed from his human spirit. His spirit retained a memory of the relationship it once enjoyed, but it was left darkened and restless, filled with both guilt and fear, and unable to contact the God it knew existed. This is why Adam and Eve immediately hid themselves. They realized they had no defense against attack and were naked. Every human being has been born into this same condition. The human spirit longs for God but is afraid to find Him. It is restless and unhappy without Him, but fearful and guilty before Him. That is the agony of fallen humanity.

The invader

When the Spirit of God was withdrawn, Adam's human spirit was left untenanted and unlighted. In this condition Adam would have been unable to move or even breathe, for God had supplied him the power to act. Spiritually, Adam was instantly cut off from God, but physically he did not die; he was able to go on living, breathing, thinking, and working. By what power? The account in Genesis does not tell us, but centuries later Paul makes it clear: Adam was instantly invaded by an alien power which took over the task of supplying the energy and impetus he needed to fulfill his choices. Adam was very likely only faintly aware of the change that came over him. Paul describes that alien power described vividly in his letter to the Ephesians:

As for you, you were dead in your transgressions and sins, in which you used to live when you followed the ways of this world and of the ruler of the kingdom of the air, the spirit who is now at work in those who are disobedient (Ephesians 2:1–2).

That power that operates universally in fallen human beings originates in some mysterious way from Satan himself. Demonic sin is intimately connected with the problem of human sin. Satan, says Paul, is "the ruler of the kingdom of the air, the spirit who is now at work in those who are disobedient." The apostle goes on to describe Satan as working out his effects through what the Bible calls "the flesh" or the "sinful nature." As Ephesians 2:3 tells us, "*All* of us also lived among them at one time, gratifying the cravings of our sinful nature and following its desires and thoughts. *Like the rest, we were by nature objects of wrath*" (emphasis added).

The emphasized words in the above passage make clear that this alien invasion is a condition common to *all* humanity. No one escapes the effects of the sin nature. Since all human beings are children of Adam by natural birth, it is also clear that this passage describes what happened to Adam in the moment of his fall. James, in his general epistle, speaks also of a wisdom that "does not come down from heaven but is earthly, unspiritual, of the devil" (James 3:15). And Jesus himself confirmed the fact that all men are born into an evil condition when He said to His disciples, "If you then, though you are evil, know how to give good gifts to your children, how much more will your Father in heaven give the Holy Spirit to those who ask him!" (Luke 11:13).

The splendor of the flesh versus the splendor of God

When we think of the devil and his relationship to God, the Bible is most careful to make clear that there are not two opposing gods, one evil and the other good. The devil, too, is a creature of God, and must live by means of the life he receives from God. There is really only one source of life in all the universe, and ultimately every living creature or spirit must derive its life from the one Author of Life, God himself. But by some means not fully revealed, the devil has interposed himself between God and humanity and takes the pure life (or love) of God and twists and distorts it so that it is no longer outward directed, as it came from God, but it becomes inward directed; that is, no longer other-loving, but it becomes self-loving. Fallen man thus receives the life of God as it has been twisted and tainted by the devil. That life is called "the flesh."

This, then, is the primary characteristic of the flesh: it is self-serving. It is God's life, misused. It can have all the outward appearance of the life of God—loving, working, forgiving, creating, serving—but with an inward motive that is aimed always and solely at the advancement of self. It thus becomes the rival of God—another god!

This is why fallen human beings, working in the energy of the flesh, can do many good deeds—good in the eyes of themselves and others around them. But God does not see them as good. He looks on the heart and not on the outward appearance, therefore He knows they are tainted right from the start. Thus Paul can say, "The mind of sinful man is death, but the mind controlled by the Spirit is life and peace; the sinful mind is hostile to God. It does not submit to God's law, nor can it do so. Those controlled by the sinful nature cannot please God" (Romans 8:6–8).

So we come out at the two splendors again. There is a certain splendid attractiveness about the flesh, trying to be good. It strongly appeals to many, but it is like the shine on Moses' face—a fading splendor! But the splendor of the new covenant is far greater. It derives from the activity of Jesus Christ at work within humanity—directly, not distorted by Satan. Thus it is perfectly acceptable to God. It is a delight to Him, for it is the activity of His beloved Son and will ever be characterized by His life—a life of genuine love, faithful work, and unreserved forgiveness; a life that is continually, freshly creative, and humbly given to service to others without thought of repayment or recognition.

That is humanity as God intended humanity to be. That is the humble yet beautiful splendor of authentic Christianity.

Death Versus Life

AT THE MOMENT YOU READ this sentence you are see-ing, reading, and thinking either in the energy of the flesh or by the energy of the Holy Spirit. To use the same visual aids employed by the apostle Paul, you are either looking at the face of Moses or you are looking at the glory of God reflected in the face of Jesus Christ. You may not be at all conscious of this, but it is true nevertheless. Furthermore, it would be equally true if you came from a remote part of the world and had never before heard of either Moses or Jesus. Every human being on this planet lives and acts according to either the old covenant or the new covenant. There is no middle ground. There is no exception. Even if you have never heard the gospel, even if you've never seen a Bible, even if you live a thousand miles from the nearest church or even the nearest Christian, Paul argues in Romans 2 that the law of God, the law of Moses, is written to some degree in your heart or conscience—and everything you do relates somehow to the law of your conscience.

The fruit reveals the root

"Well," you may say, "if one is hardly conscious of which face you are looking at in any given moment, how can you know when you are in the flesh and when you are in the Spirit?" The answer: By the quality of "fruit" your life produces! The flesh invariably produces one kind of life; the Spirit invariably produces another kind. Jesus has this truth in mind when He says: "By their fruit you will recognize them" (Matthew 7:20).

Before we go on to look at Paul's practical description of these two kinds of living, we should remind ourselves that until we become born again as Christians, we have no choice but to live by the flesh and produce the life of the flesh. The "good" that may be in our lives is but an imitation good that comes from the flesh's effort to fulfill the law of God. As hard as it may be to believe, this kind of fleshly "good" is really no better in God's sight than the evil manifested by the flesh. It is only disguised evil.

On the other hand, to be born again supplies the mere possibility of living in the Spirit; it does not make authentic spiritual living automatic. The true Christian can, and often does, manifest the phony righteousness of the flesh, though one can also (and does, as he learns to live by faith) manifest the wholesome qualities of the Spirit.

Paul shows us a remarkable series of four contrasts in 2 Corinthians 3:7–11, so we can distinguish the result of trusting in the flesh from the result of trusting in the Spirit in our daily lives. When we learn to recognize which force is at work within us, then we will be ready to change from the flesh to the Spirit.

First, Paul contrasts the immediate effect produced by the flesh with that produced by the Spirit: "Now if the ministry that brought death, which was engraved in letters on stone, came with glory, so that the Israelites could not look steadily at the face of Moses because of its glory, fading though it was, will not the ministry of the Spirit be even more glorious?" (2 Corinthians 3:7–8).

The flesh produces death, the Spirit produces life! Paul has already pointed it out in verse 6: "for the letter kills, but the Spirit gives life." One is a dispensation of death, the other is a dispensation of greater splendor, a dispensation of life. The word *dispensation* is helpful if we understand it in its original sense: to dispense or produce. If we think of a dispensation as a period of time, it will be confusing to use the word here. In fact, a much better word might be *ministry.* The Greek is *diakonia,* which is usually translated ministry or service. What is being dispensed in the ministry of the Spirit? It is life! To depend on everything coming from you, in response to the demand of the law, produces immediate death. To depend on everything coming from God produces immediate life.

To think of death in terms of a funeral, as the end of existence, is to miss the point of what Paul is saying here. What is death? It is essentially a negative term meaning the absence of life. A doctor who examines an injured person does not look for signs of death; he checks for the signs of life. If he does not find them, he knows the man is dead. Life produces its own distinctive marks; death is the absence of those marks. That being so, the question we must really ask is: What is life?

Well, sometimes we hear a person say, "Man, I'm really living!" What does that person mean? That he or she is experiencing great *enjoyment,* of course! Enjoyment is a part of life, as God intended it to be. Purpose, meaning, worth, fulfillment; all these are part of life. How about other qualities—joy, peace, love, friendship, power? Yes, that's abundant life. The moment we have these qualities, we are *living*. Surely, this is what Jesus meant when He said, "I have come that they may have life, and have it to the full" (John 10:10). That is Life with a capital *L*. Life lived to the full—full of love, joy, peace, long-suffering, gentleness, goodness, faith, meekness, self-control—man, that's living!

In contrast then, what is death? It is the absence or opposite of those qualities of life. What is the absence of love? Hate, selfishness, and fear. What is the absence of joy? Misery, weariness of spirit, anger, hopelessness. Thus frustration, boredom, worry, hostility, jealousy, malice, loneliness, depression, self-pity—these are all marks of the absence of life. In short, they are forms of death. We do not need to wait till we die to experience these. For all too many of us, they are a major part of our experience while we yet live. They represent death in the midst of life.

The source of death

Where do these attitudes and passions come from, often when we least expect them? Jesus helps us answer these questions. "Do people pick grapes from thornbushes, or figs from thistles? Likewise every good tree bears good fruit, but a bad tree bears bad fruit. A good tree cannot bear bad fruit, and a bad tree cannot bear good fruit" (Matthew 7:16–18). We think these negative qualities come from passing moods or changing circumstances. Both Jesus and Paul say, no! They come from something deeper, something much more fundamental. They arise from a dependence on the old covenant, the "bad tree" that cannot produce good fruit. They reveal that we are unconsciously or consciously depending on "something coming from me" rather than "everything coming from God."

These negative feelings, then, reveal the flesh in action. Not the flesh in the blatant display of evil that we usually think of—drunkenness, rioting, adultery, thievery, murder, and the like—but the flesh in those subtler displays we often approve and even seek after: self-sufficiency, self-pity, self-centeredness. This is why every biblical counselor learns to look beyond the immediate manifestation of hostility, depression, boredom, and to seek the root causes that drive these feelings.

For instance, I have learned in my own life (and also by observing others) that depression is usually caused by some form of self-pity. I become depressed because I suffer some disappointment or rejection and this causes me to feel sorry for myself. I want to be admired. I want someone to focus attention on me, and when this doesn't happen, I become depressed.

Where does loneliness come from? Most frequently from some form of self-ministry, taking care of myself only. That is why the cure for loneliness is Jesus' word: "I tell you the truth, unless a kernel of wheat falls to the ground and dies, it remains only a single seed." In other words, it becomes lonely. Loneliness is the inevitable result of clutching and clinging to self, and refusing to die to self. Jesus continues: "But if it dies, it produces many seeds" (John 12:24).

The presence of these marks of death gives us the clue as to when the old covenant is at work. Whenever these negative qualities are there, the old covenant is working, for that is what produces them. On the other hand, whenever the qualities of joy, trust, confidence, beauty, worth, and fulfillment are present, they can only come from the new covenant. It is the Spirit of God who produces them.

Paul reminds us that there are two glories or splendors involved here. There is a certain glory about the "death" which the old covenant produces, but there is a greater glory about life. There is a certain attractiveness about the marks of death. We take a morbid pleasure in them. Have you ever caught yourself wallowing in a morass of self-pity and resisting all attempts to bring you out of it? You wanted to be let alone so you could have a good time feeling sorry for yourself. It gives a perverse feeling of pleasure. James says, "Such 'wisdom' does not come down from heaven but is earthly, unspiritual, of the devil. For where you have envy and selfish ambition, there you find disorder and every evil practice" (James 3:15–16).

The amazing thing is that we prefer these temporary, fleeting pleasures to the glory that accompanies real life. Often, we naively assume we can enjoy both. But if we insist on having the momentary pleasure that comes from the old covenant, then we cannot have the lasting pleasure that comes from the new covenant. No one can serve two masters, remember? So the first contrast the apostle draws, by which we can recognize the old or new covenants in action, is that of the immediate effects produced in life.

Stones or hearts?

The second contrast is associated with the first. It has to do with the material substance with which each is concerned. In 2 Corinthians 3:3 the apostle has already referred to these differences. The new covenant, he says, is "written not with ink but with the Spirit of the living God, not on tablets of stone but on tablets of human hearts." Twice in this passage he stresses the medium by which the old covenant came: "Now if the ministry that brought death, which was engraved in letters on stone, came with glory . . ." (verse 7). The law was written on stones; the Spirit writes on human hearts. The old covenant is concerned with stones, with dead things; the new covenant is concerned with hearts, with living people.

One mark, therefore, of *false* Christianity is that it is always deeply concerned with the importance of *things:* stones, rituals, ceremonies, buildings, stained-glass windows, spires, organs, proper procedures. The emphasis is put on these at the expense of people. But the new covenant reverses this emphasis. People are the important matter. Things are useful only as they help or do not help people.

Look at Jesus. See how utterly careless He was about the precise regulations of the Pharisees when those regulations stood in the way of healing people. Even the Sabbath was set aside when it stood in the way of meeting the needs of people. Jesus said that His disciples ate grain on the Sabbath because the Sabbath was made for man, not man for the Sabbath. The ultimate concern of the new covenant is always for people. The old covenant puts things first.

A number of years ago, a church in California hired a young man to "reach youth and bring them into the church." He was so successful that soon the auditorium of the church was filled with young people—but in the eyes of the church elders they were the *wrong* young people, because they were for the most part "street people" with bare feet, bizarre clothing, and untraditional ways. Eventually the youth leader was dismissed because, as he was told, "You are bringing this trash from the streets into our nice sanctuary." That is an extreme form of the old covenant in action.

The world of business and politics almost always operates on the basis of the old covenant. That is why money is usually more important than people. When vested interests are at stake, the rights of people usually suffer. Let a company face a drop in sales or production and what happens? Management takes up the axe and heads begin to roll, with little regard as to how those people will survive. Profits come first. And how much of this attitude is also seen in the church! Reputations often come before people. Programs and customs are perpetuated, not because they meet needs, but because status and acceptance are at stake—a dead giveaway that dependence is on "everything coming from us" rather than "everything coming from God."

Guilt or righteousness?

A third contrast, found in 2 Corinthians 3:9, marks the difference between freedom and guilt: "If the ministry that condemns men is glorious, how much more glorious is the ministry that brings righteousness!" Here we find another mark of the old covenant in action. It inevitably produces a sense of condemnation—or to use a more modern term, *guilt.* But the new covenant produces quite the reverse: The feeling engendered is one of righteousness.

Unfortunately, "righteousness" is one of those great biblical words that is often misunderstood today. Most of us think of it as "doing what is right," and certainly that is part of its meaning. But the essence of the term goes much deeper. Its basic meaning is "being what is right." One *does* what is right, because one *is* right—that is the biblical idea of righteousness. Righteousness is the quality of being acceptable to and accepted by God—fully and without reserve.

Perhaps we will get the true sense of it if we substitute the word "worth." The righteous person is the one who has a sense of being valued. He is no longer troubled with guilt, inadequacy, or hostility. He does not strive to produce something to earn significance, for he feels accepted by God, pleasing to God. Therefore this person is free to reach out to others who hurt or are fearful or feel condemned because he is free of these feelings. To depend on "everything coming from God, nothing coming from me" produces that sense of worth. That is righteousness.

On the other hand, how many Christians live continually under a sense of condemnation? When the basis for our Christian activity is dependence on something coming from us (our personality, our willpower, our gifts, our money, our courage), there is no escape from a sense of guilt, for we can never be certain when we have done enough! Around the world that basis of performance is driving Christians into frenetic activity that can result in nothing but sheer exhaustion.

I was once in an American city where a woman stood up and told how her performance was being challenged in her church, and she confessed how inadequate and threatened she felt. She was almost in tears, feeling she had not done enough for God, not knowing what else to do. The despair she exemplified is a far cry from the joyful word of Romans 8:1–2, "There is now no condemnation for those who are in Christ Jesus, because through Christ Jesus the law of the Spirit of life set me free from the law of sin and death." How much this woman needed to see that God already loved her as much as He ever will, and nothing she could ever do, or not do, would change that. To really believe this truth would make her free to "do"—not in order to win acceptance, but because she was already pleasing to God.

The frenzied activities of Christians have become a joke. Someone has revised the old nursery rhyme to read:

Mary had a little lamb,
'Twas given her to keep;
But then it joined the Baptist Church,
And died for lack of sleep!

Many churches judge their success by the number of activities they offer. For many, it comes as a great shock to learn from Scripture that a church can be an utter failure before God and yet be occupied to the full every night of the week—teaching the right doctrines and doing the right things. On the other hand, a church whose people are living by the new covenant can also be fully occupied with many and varied activities. It is not the *level* of activity that marks the success or failure of a church. It is the *source* of that activity. Is it the flesh, or the Spirit? Is it *my* background, *my* training, *my* education, *my* personality? Or is it God—at work in me through Jesus Christ?

Surpassing glory

Remember, there is a certain glory about the activity of the flesh that is very attractive to people. Dedicated activity always gives one a certain sense of worth—for awhile! It produces a kind of self-approval that is very pleasant to experience—for awhile. Paul says that "the ministry that brought death, which was engraved in letters on stone, came with glory" (2 Corinthians 3:7), yet it is far surpassed by the glory and splendor of the ministry of righteousness. In fact, the apostle enlarges on this. He says, "If the ministry that condemns men is glorious, how much more glorious is the ministry that brings righteousness! *For what was glorious has no glory now in comparison with the surpassing glory*" (2 Corinthians 3:9–10, emphasis added).

This is undoubtedly an oblique reference to Paul's own experience which we have already traced in a previous chapter. The pleasure he derived from his dependence upon his ancestry, his orthodoxy, his morality, and his activity soon came to have "no glory now in comparison with the surpassing glory." To trust in Jesus Christ, at work in him, as he describes it in Galatians 2:20, is to experience a sense of fulfillment and worth that is infinitely beyond anything he had ever experienced before. It was to be free! Little did he care what men thought of him, since he was so fully aware of what God thought of him—in Christ. Little did he care what appraisal men (even other Christians) might make of his ministry, since he fully understood that whatever Christ did through him would be approved in the eyes of God. That is why he was able to say, "Always give yourselves fully to the work of the Lord, because you know that your labor in the Lord is not in vain" (1 Corinthians 15:58).

Fading or permanent?

The final contrast Paul draws relates closely to the previous one. He says, "If what was fading away came with glory, how much greater is the glory of that which lasts!" (2 Corinthians 3:11). The contrast is clear. The old covenant produces that which fades away, but the new produces that which is permanent. When Moses came down from the mountain with his face aglow, he found that the glory faded. Relatively soon it disappeared completely, never to be recovered. But the glory of Jesus' face never changes. Those who are expecting him to be at work through them in response to the demands that normal living makes upon them will experience *eternal* results. They will never fade or lose their value. They are treasure laid up in heaven—not on earth.

Death Versus Life   79

Once again Paul reminds us of the attractiveness that accompanies dependence upon the flesh. Challenging people to rely on their natural resources and abilities can often whip up a tremendous wave of excitement and enthusiasm. From such a meeting everyone goes home saying, "Wow, what a tremendous meeting! I can't wait to get started on this new program. This year we are going to make it." But every experienced leader knows what will happen. Soon the enthusiasm will begin to ebb—it might not last beyond the next morning! Those who go around later to collect on some of the promises made will find that people have grown dull and apathetic. By next year it must all be done over again, with new approaches and more powerful presentations, in order to stir up the same degree of excitement and commitment. Sound familiar?

"But," you might say, "that's just human nature. It is only realism to take it into consideration and make plans to overcome such apathy." This statement is true—it is human nature. But it is *fallen* human nature: in other words, the flesh!

But have you ever met anyone who has learned to function on the basis of the new covenant? They don't need repeated meetings to whip up their enthusiasm. After twenty-five years they're still just as fresh and vital on the same job as they were the day they started.

I once met an old man who had been a missionary to the loggers in the backwoods of British Columbia for forty years. Recently he had been retired by his mission, but his zeal and enthusiasm for the Lord's work were unflagging. He had never grown weary of his work, though he was often weary in it, and if the mission would let him, he wanted to go back to the woods again with confidence and courage, knowing that the Lord who worked through him was perfectly adequate for whatever would happen.

The new covenant refreshes the spirit continually. When the human spirit weakens in the face of continued demand (as intended), it looks immediately to the indwelling God, to the Fountain of Living Water, receiving vigor and vitality to meet the day's demands with eagerness and enthusiasm. People who live on that basis are a delight to work with. They do not require continual encouragement and outward motivation (though they fully appreciate the kind words people say to them), for they know the secret of their activity is "nothing coming from me but everything from God." That permanent glory never fades. The activity of the flesh is always a fading glory.

The big push

With these four contrasts Paul seeks to impress us with the total inadequacy of the flesh, despite appearances, and the total adequacy of the Spirit, despite the evaluations of men, whether of ourselves or others. It is the energy of the flesh versus the power of the Spirit of life in Christ Jesus, as Paul puts it in Romans 8. If, as a Christian, you are seeking to live by your own resources rather than by the life of Jesus within you, you are like a man who goes down to buy a car and does not know that it comes equipped with a motor. Naturally, a man buying a car on that basis would have to push it home. When he gets there, he might invite his family out for a ride, so the wife gets in behind the wheel, the kids in the back seat, and he starts pushing from behind. At that point you might come along and ask, "How do you like your car?"

"Oh, it is a tremendous car. Look at the upholstery, and get an eyeful of this color, and, oh yes, listen to the horn—what a great horn this car has. But, I do find it rather exhausting! It goes downhill beautifully, but if there is even the slightest rise in the pavement, I find myself panting and struggling and groaning. It is very difficult to push it uphill."

"Well, my friend," you may say, "you do need help. You know, at our church we are having special meetings this week. Our speaker is speaking on the very subject you need to hear: 'How to Push a Car Successfully!' On Monday night he is going to show us how to push with the right shoulder. On Tuesday night he will illustrate the techniques of pushing with the left shoulder. On Wednesday night he has colored slides and an overhead projector to show us how to really get our back into the work and push. On Thursday night he has committees and workshops organized that will help us all push more effectively, and on Friday night there will be a great dedication service where we all come down in front to commit ourselves anew to the work of pushing cars. Come every night next week, and learn all there is to know about how to push a car successfully!"

That is exactly the way many Christians live today. We spend hours seeking to teach people how to mobilize all their human resources and try harder to get the job done for God. But all we are mobilizing is the flesh. We seek to build up their confidence in the power of numbers, the hidden resources of the human spirit, and the possibilities of a determined will.

But if we really wanted to help the man who is pushing his car, we would say something like this. "Look, come around here in front." We would lift up the hood and say to him, "Do you see this iron thing with all the wiggles coming out of it? Do you know what that is? It's a motor. A power plant. The maker of this car knew you would have the problem that you've been having and so he designed a power plant that would enable you to go uphill as easily as downhill. When you learn several simple things about operating the motor, you will begin to experience the power. Just turn this key and the motor will start. Then you pull down that lever and step on the pedal on the floor and away you go. You do the steering, but the motor supplies *all* the power. You don't have to push at all. Just sit back and you can go up the highest hills with as much ease and relaxation as if you were going downhill. You don't need to worry for the motor is equal to whatever demand you make."

Now that is what authentic Christianity is all about. God knew that we human beings aren't adequate in ourselves to meet the demands life makes upon us so He supplied a power plant—the life of Jesus Himself. It is perfectly adequate for the task. Our part is to learn to operate it correctly, then make the choices necessary to steering. When we do, we experience the restfulness of activity in His strength. That is, indeed, a surpassing glory!

Let's get going

Perhaps many of you feel you would like to quit reading at this point. The truth you have already learned is so exhilarating that you're anxious to stop reading and start living. I don't blame you. The adventure of new covenant living is wonderful to experience. But the Apostle Paul does not let us go at this point. He has much more to say, and what he says is absolutely necessary to experiencing what God has for us.

VI

The Enemy Within

THOMAS CRANMER—archbishop of Canterbury during the middle sixteenth century—was noted for promoting the Reformation in England, for disseminating the Coverdale English Bible, and for creating the liturgy of the Anglican Church. He repudiated the rule of the pope in Rome and attempted to bring about a union between the Church of England and the Lutheran church of Germany.

Later, when Mary Tudor—a devout Roman Catholic—became queen of England, Cranmer was arrested and imprisoned in the Tower of London. He was convicted of both treason and heresy, and was deprived of sleep and subjected to almost continuous questioning, brow-beating, and haranguing for several weeks. He was often threatened with torture and death. Under this pressure, Cranmer signed a series of confessions, in which he recanted his earlier support for the Reformation, his proclaiming of salvation by grace through faith, and his belief that the Scriptures belonged to all the people, not just the Catholic clergy.

Even though he signed the recantations that were demanded of him, and despite promises made to him that these signed documents would save him from torture and death, the papers were presented as evidence against him in a final trial for treason. The court condemned him to death by burning at the stake—but told him the sentence would not be carried out if he made a public recantation of his former beliefs. He was taken before a large crowd at St. Mary's Church, Oxford, to confess his former errors—but instead of confessing, he declared, "My conscience will not let me deny the truth any longer, even to save my life. I have signed seven recantations of the truth, and I bitterly regret each one. I abhor my right hand for signing those recantations, and when they take me to the flames, I shall hold my right hand steadfastly in the flames."

The authorities stopped him in mid-speech, dragged him out of the church, and took him away to be executed. As the fire was being prepared, he trusted God to give him the strength to keep his promise, and he boldly thrust his right hand into the flames. Then he was bound to the stake, surrounded with wood, and put to a martyr's death.

Boldness! That is the inevitable result of trust in God, trust in the new covenant—everything coming from God, nothing coming from me. Boldness, courage, and confidence, of course, are just what people everywhere are searching for. They instinctively know that effective action must issue from a courageous, confident spirit. They try in a thousand ways to summon up that confidence from within, but they are looking in the wrong place. There is a form of boldness they can find in themselves, but it will end as a fading glory.

But that is not the source of Paul's boldness! He has found the secret of *true* boldness. His basis is different. "Therefore," says Paul in 2 Corinthians 3:12, "since we have such a hope, we are very bold." That is Paul's triumphant conclusion to his discussion of the two covenants at work in humanity. His boldness is rooted in a sure hope, a conviction that God is ready to work in him.

All who trust in this hope become noticeably bold. Because they are not trusting in themselves or in some effort they are making on behalf of God but on God Himself, they can be supremely confident. And since success does not depend any longer on their own dedication, zeal, wisdom, background or training, then they can be very bold. It is God who will do it, and He can be depended upon not to fail—though He very well may take some unexpected route to accomplish His ends.

When we can trust God to work in any given situation, He delivers us completely from the fear of failure. At that moment, what else can we be but invincibly bold!

When Moses was afraid

Paul immediately goes on to say, "We are not like Moses, who would put a veil over his face to keep the Israelites from gazing at it while the radiance was fading away" (2 Corinthians 3:13). On at least one occasion Moses was not bold. He was, indeed, the very opposite! He was fearful and threatened.

Here we learn something about Moses that the Old Testament does not reveal. In the Old Testament account, Moses was not aware of the shining of his face when he came down from Mt. Sinai. Naturally it didn't take him long to learn that something unusual was happening when people closed their eyes or shielded their faces in his presence. It actually became necessary for Moses to cover his face with a veil when he talked to people. There was nothing wrong with that. It was perfectly proper, in view of the circumstances. But Moses soon knew something that the people of Israel didn't know: The glory was fading.

At first Moses put on the veil every morning because of the brightness of his face. But as time passed and the brightness faded to nothing more than a dim glow, he still wore the veil each day.

Now Paul raises the question: *Why?* Why did Moses keep the veil on his face after the glory had faded? His answer: Moses was *afraid.* Afraid of what? Afraid that the Israelites would see that the glory had faded! The mark of his privilege and status before God was disappearing, and Moses did not want anyone to know it. So he did what millions have done ever since, he hid the fact of his faded glory behind a facade, a veil. He did not let anyone see what was really going on inside.

The veil of pride

It is clear that Paul uses this veil over Moses' face as a symbol of a further activity of the flesh, for he finds the same veil still around in his own day. The Jews of his time were a continuing example. He writes:

> Their minds were made dull, for to this day the same veil remains when the old covenant is read. It has not been removed, because only in Christ is it taken away. Even to this day when Moses is read, a veil covers their hearts. But whenever anyone turns to the Lord, the veil is taken away (2 Corinthians 3:14–16).

When Moses brought the Ten Commandments down from the mountain, he read them to the people. Their immediate response was: "We will do everything the LORD has said." The confidence and pride of the flesh rose up as if to say, "We've got what it takes to do everything you say, God. Don't worry about us. We are your faithful people, and whatever you say, we will do." The truth was, of course, that before the day was over they had broken all ten of the commandments. They knew it, but they didn't want anyone else to know. So they put up a facade. They covered over their failure with religious ritual and convinced themselves that the ritual was all God wanted. The pride that would not admit failure was the veil that hid the end of the fading glory. They could not see the death that was waiting at the end. And they could not feel the frustration and defeat that would be theirs when the flesh had finished its fatal work.

Fifteen hundred years after Moses, Paul found the same veil at work in Israel. The Jews of his day made the same response to the demands of the law as their forefathers had made at Mt. Sinai: they promised to obey. Now, two thousand years after Paul the same phenomenon is occurring. When some demand is made upon the natural life, its response is, "All right, I'll do it," or at least, "I'll try." Even in Christians, the confidence that they can do something for God blinds their eyes to the end of the fading glory. They believe that something good can be accomplished if they just give it the old college try. So today that same veil remains unlifted.

False fronts

Veils come in many forms today, but they are always essentially the same: An image or front we present to others, and behind which we hide our real selves. They are always, therefore, a form of pride and hypocrisy. We don't want people to see our fading glory. Actually, we are reluctant to admit it has happened, even to ourselves. And by wearing our veils long enough we are in great danger of beginning to believe that we are the kind of people we want everyone to think we are. Then we become blind to our hypocrisy and its perpetuation is assured. This is that subtle deceitfulness of the heart which Jeremiah saw so clearly and lamented: "The heart is deceitful above all things and beyond cure. Who can understand it?" (Jeremiah 17:9).

Yes, the veils we employ are unbelievably varied. Pride has a thousand faces. It is a master of disguise. C. S. Lewis has rightly said,

> There is one vice of which no man in the world is free; which everyone in the world loathes when he sees it in someone else; and of which hardly any people, except Christians, ever imagine that they are guilty themselves. . . . There is no fault which makes a man more unpopular, and no fault which we are more unconscious of in ourselves. And the more we have it ourselves, the more we dislike it in others. The vice I am talking of is Pride or Self-Conceit; and the virtue opposite to it, in Christian morals, is called Humility (*Mere Christianity*, p. 106).

Yet despite the unpopularity pride creates for us, these apparently innocent veils are so necessary to our ego support that we invent many clever ways to preserve them. One is to have a "double entry" system of names. When a form of pride becomes evident in others, we have one name for it; when the same thing characterizes us, we have a nicer name for it. Others have prejudices; we have convictions. Others are conceited; we have self-respect. Others garishly keep up with the Joneses; we simply try to get ahead. Others blow up, or lose their tempers; we are seized with righteous indignation.

C. S. Lewis suggests that only Christians become aware of pride in themselves. Certainly it is true that most non-Christians, if they see pride in themselves at all, regard it as a virtue rather than a vice. But unfortunately, being a Christian does not guarantee easy recognition of all forms of pride. Christians are particularly susceptible to donning certain veils, especially those that seem to be forms of Christian virtue.

Take false modesty, for example. I learned long ago that when I hear some Christian say, "I'm only trying to serve the Lord in my own humble way," I'm probably talking to the proudest person in six counties! St. Jerome warned: "Beware of the pride of humility." I once heard of a congregation who gave their pastor a medal for humility—then took it away because he wore it! True humility, of course, is never aware of itself. It is most noteworthy that the greatest saints have been most aware of their pride. And the truly humble person would never see this virtue in himself. Pious language is a dead giveaway of towering pride.

Veils Christians wear

Then there is self-righteousness. This is a particularly noxious form of Christian pride. It seizes upon some biblical standard of conduct and takes pride in its own ability to measure up externally while conveniently overlooking any failure of the inner or thought life to conform. The end result is a smug, patronizing, and even nasty attitude toward anyone who does not meet the standard. This is the sin Jesus struck at most forcibly. He exposed it in the Pharisees and said that even the adulterers and the extortioners would enter the kingdom of heaven before them. It is the sin of the crusader who habitually mounts a white horse and rides out to combat any form of evil he considers reprehensible.

Self-righteousness is also the sin of the person who nags another, for the nagger is focusing on a single point of conduct and ignores the areas in his or her own life where a similar failure is occurring. Instinctively, we retreat behind this veil whenever failure or weakness is exposed in us. ("I may be weak there, but at least I don't do such-and-such.") We keep self-righteous veils always close at hand so they can be put on quickly to keep others from seeing the end of the fading glory.

Another common Christian veil is sensitivity or touchiness. People who are touchy or excessively sensitive are easily hurt by the words or actions of others. They must be handled with kid gloves lest they take offense. And when offended, they suffer agonies of spirit and tend to wallow in a morass of self-pity for hours, or even days, on end. Their explanation of such agony is always the "thoughtlessness" or "rudeness" of others, but in reality it is their own protest at not being given the attention or prominence which they're sure they deserve. Years ago a wise Christian woman summed it up for me in a brief statement I'll never forget. "I've learned," she said, "that sensitivity is nothing but selfishness." That helped greatly to free me from a struggle I was having with touchiness at the time.

An impatient spirit can be a veil to hide the reality of what we are. It is often manifested to indicate importance or busyness. It frequently appears as a mark of zeal or dedication. But to be easily irritated, to frown readily, or reply sharply is a form of pride usually used to cover insecurity or a deep sense of inferiority. A self-justifying habit reveals something similar. Those people who can't stand to be misunderstood but are forever explaining their actions are really saying, "I want you to think I'm perfect. Of course, I know that the present situation does not let me appear so, but if you will just let me explain . . ." It is no wonder this habit is frequently associated with what is called perfectionism.

But perhaps the most common veil employed by Christians is remoteness: the practice of keeping feelings and attitudes completely to oneself, even with friends or close relatives. Remoteness arises primarily from fear—the fear of being known for what one is. Often, though, it is described defensively as "reserve," "privacy," or "reticence." It is clearly a veil to keep others from seeing a fading glory and is a direct violation of such biblical commands as "confess your sins to each other and pray for each other so that you may be healed" (James 5:16) and "Carry each other's burdens, and in this way you will fulfill the law of Christ" (Galatians 6:2). After all, how can another bear your burden if you don't share it?

All of these commands are summed up in the direct and repeated command of Jesus, "Love each other" (John 15:12), which He goes on to define as including, among other elements, the sharing of secrets (see John 15:15). Paul tells the Corinthian believers (in 2 Corinthians 6:11) that he has opened his heart fully to them and exhorts them: "As a fair exchange—I speak as to my children—open wide your hearts also" (2 Corinthians 6:13).

The big lie

It is apparent from the above examples that the flesh, or natural life, likes nothing better than to hide or disguise itself. We all tend to fear rejection if we are seen for what we are. The satanic lie is that in order to be liked or accepted we must appear capable or successful. Therefore we either project capability (the extrovert) or we seek to hide our failure (the introvert). The new covenant offers the opposite. If we will admit our inadequacy, we can have God's adequacy, and all we have sought vainly to produce (confidence, success, impact, integrity, and reality) is given to us at the point of our inability. The key is to take away the veil.

A modern songwriter, John Fischer, has captured, with delicious humor, the tendency of evangelical Christians to wear veils. Enjoy a good laugh at your own expense.

Evangelical Veil Productions

Evangelical Veil Productions!
Pick one up at quite a reduction;
Got all kinds of shapes and sizes;
Introductory bonus prizes!
Special quality, one-way see through;
You can see them but they can't see you.
Never have to show yourself again!

Just released—A Moses model;
Comes with shine in a plastic bottle,
It makes you look like you've just seen the Lord!
Just one daily application
And you'll fool the congregation,
Guaranteed to last a whole week through.

Got a Back-from-the-Summer-Camp veil,
With a Mountain-top look that'll never fail,
As long as you renew it every year.
Lots of special Jesus freak files,
every one comes with a permanent smile,
One-way button, and a sticker for your car.

(*Repeat first verse—then shout:*)
YOU'RE PROTECTED!

(*Used by permission*)

The great unveiling

How can these veils be removed? The answer is clearly stated by Paul in the Scripture passage we are considering:

> Their minds were made dull, for to this day the same veil remains when the old covenant is read. It has not been removed, because *only in Christ is it taken away*. Even to this day when Moses is read, a veil covers their hearts. But whenever anyone turns to the Lord, *the veil is taken away* (2 Corinthians 3:14–16, emphasis added).

Only in Christ is the veil taken away! And as the apostle goes on to tell us, "Now the Lord is the Spirit, and where the Spirit of the Lord is, there is freedom" (verse 17). Here is our first real key in moving from the old covenant to the new. The key is the Spirit. Some may be confused by Paul's word that only through Christ can the veil be taken away. They may wonder, "Are we to turn to the Spirit or to Christ to have the veil removed?" The answer, of course, is that it makes no difference.

In Scripture, the Holy Spirit is frequently called the Spirit of Christ. It is His divine task and joy to enter the life of those who believe in Jesus and continually unleash in them the very life of Jesus Himself. Thus, to turn to the Spirit is also to turn to Christ. It is by means of the Spirit that we turn to Christ.

We must further see that in practical terms "to turn to the Spirit" means to have faith in the promise of the Spirit, to trust the word of God. It is to expect the Spirit to act in line with what He has said He will do. Specifically, the promise is to apply to our practical, daily lives the full value of both the death and the resurrection of Jesus. His death has cut us off from our old, natural life, as Paul tells us in Romans 6:6—"We know that our old self was crucified with him so that the body of sin might be rendered powerless, that we should no longer be slaves to sin."

When we agree with this word concerning the specific form of pride we are at the moment experiencing (that is, the particular veil we are hiding behind), we are immediately freed by the Spirit from its control. We have called the veil what God calls it, which is usually also what we call it when we find it in someone else. It can no longer be excused or justified— we repudiate it, and the fleeting pleasure it offers us. That is what it means to turn to the Spirit. As Paul describes it,"if *by the Spirit* you put to death the misdeeds of the body, you will live (Romans 8:13, emphasis added). Remember, when we turn to the Lord, the veil is removed—and the Lord is the Spirit.

Free to live

The second function of the Spirit is to make real to us in practical terms the resurrection of Jesus, as well as His death. This is the second part of "turning to the Lord." The first act of the Spirit ends the reign of the old life over us. The second act releases to us the resurrected life of Jesus. That is what the Scripture calls *freedom.* "Now the Lord is the Spirit," says verse 17, "and where the Spirit of the Lord is, there is freedom."

When by faith in that promise we have turned from the flesh with its lying promise of success and have trusted in the Lord Jesus, dwelling within us by His Spirit, to be ready to work the moment we choose to act, we have in very practical terms passed from the old covenant to the new. Nothing coming from us, everything coming from God! That is freedom!

The apostle goes on to describe this freedom in glorious terms: "We, who with unveiled faces all reflect the Lord's glory, are being transformed into his likeness with ever-increasing glory, which comes from the Lord, who is the Spirit" (2 Corinthians 3:18). Note the term *unveiled faces.* By faith in the promise of God (that is, by the Spirit) we have ceased to look at the face of Moses and are now beholding with full vision "the glory of God in the face of Christ" (4:6). The veil is removed. Moses and the law are gone; only Jesus Christ fills the horizon of our life—for that precise moment.

It is altogether possible that a minute or two later we may, like Peter walking on the water, take our eyes off Jesus' face and begin to look once again at our circumstances and our limited resources. At that moment, of course, Moses and the law return. The *temptation* to do this is not the act, and we can find our faith sorely tested while still having it fixed upon the face of Jesus. But when we succumb to these pressures and begin to trust ourselves or others, we are back in the old covenant, wearing a veil over our faces, and must repeat the whole process for deliverance.

God is not angry

But let us not despair or feel condemned when this happens. Remember that God has already made full provision for failure in learning to live by the Spirit. He anticipates our struggles and our defeats and only expects us to recognize them as well and return immediately to the principle of the new covenant. God is not angry with us or upset because we have fallen. We are angry at ourselves, perhaps, but that only shows us more fully how much we were expecting something to come from us. We need but to thank God for letting us see what we were unwittingly trusting in and then resume our confidence that Jesus is at work in us as we take up the task at hand again.

This continual return to beholding the glory of the Lord is doing something to us, says Paul. More and more areas of our conscious experience (our soul) are coming under the full control of the Spirit, and we are therefore reflecting an increasing likeness to Jesus; we are being changed into His likeness from one degree of glory to another. This is what we often call "Christian growth" or "growing in grace." Because of constant practice of the principle of the new covenant, it is increasingly easy to keep the eyes of the heart fixed on the face of Jesus. Gradually it feels more and more "natural" to walk in the Spirit and not in the flesh. The writer of Hebrews speaks of those "who by constant use have trained themselves to distinguish good from evil" (Hebrews 5:14). It is still possible, under sufficient provocation or allurement, to act in the flesh in any given relationship of life, but it is increasingly unlikely, for the heart is being "strengthened by grace" (Hebrews 13:9).

Though this gracious effect is occurring in certain areas of the conscious life, it has not yet conquered all the areas in which we live. "Glory," the glory of the life of Jesus, is becoming dominant in some areas, but in others the flesh still reigns triumphant and must be attacked and subdued by the Spirit so that another degree of glory may become evident. What is happening has often been pictured as a throne room in the heart, where at first ego (symbolized by the letter E) is seated upon the throne, and Christ (symbolized by the cross) is waiting to be given his rightful place of rule, as in the illustration below.

When the human will (the throne) is submitted to the authority of Christ, the ego is cast off the throne and Christ rules as Lord in the heart, as illustrated below:

Growth is a process

These diagrams have been helpful to many, but are inadequate, for they represent the human heart as a single entity and the will as a single factor governing the whole of the inner life at one time. I believe it is more accurate to recognize the word *heart*, commonly employed in Scripture, as referring to the soul and spirit combined, as below:

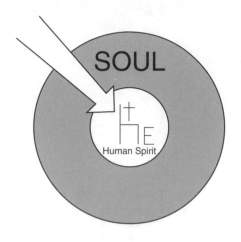

THE SPIRIT OF GOD PENETRATES THE
HUMAN SPIRIT: EGO IS DETHRONED

Note in this illustration that at the conversion of the individual, the Spirit of God penetrates the human spirit, dethrones the ego (or the flesh), and replaces it with the cross, depicting the life of Jesus. But that is *only* within the human *spirit*. The *soul* is still under the control of the *flesh* and remains so until the Spirit successively invades each area or relationship and establishes the lordship of Jesus within. This is important to understand: *There is a throne in every area of the human soul!* The question of lordship is fought out anew in each area, as indicated in the next illustration.

The up-and-down life

This would explain why it is possible for an individual Christian to be in the Spirit one moment and in the flesh the next. A good biblical example of this is in Matthew 16:16 where Peter confesses to Jesus, "You are the Christ, the Son of the living God." To this, Jesus replies, "Blessed are you, Simon son of Jonah, for this

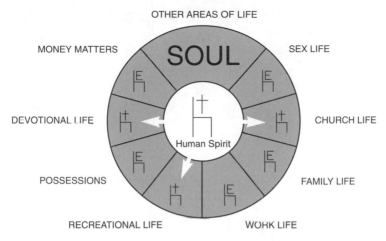

THE HOLY SPIRIT INVADES AREAS OF THE SOUL

† = THE LORDSHIP OF CHRIST
E = EGO, OR FLESH, IN CONTROL

was not revealed to you by man, but by my Father in heaven." It is clear here that Peter spoke in the Spirit when he made his confession of the identity of Jesus.

However, in verse 22 of the same account, Peter actually rebukes Jesus for suggesting that He will be crucified and resurrected again. To this rebuke Jesus says, "Get behind me, Satan! You are a stumbling block to me; you do not have in mind the things of God, but the things of men." Here Peter speaks from the flesh in ignorant opposition to the will and purpose of God.

It is evident that when it was a question of Peter's rational acceptance or rejection of Jesus' *identity*, the Spirit had already successfully enthroned Jesus as Lord in that area of Peter's life. But when it came to the matter of Peter's *involvement* with the program of crucifixion and resurrection made necessary by that identification, the flesh was still very much on the

The Enemy Within   101

throne and Jesus was not yet Lord of that area. But that was all in the realm of Peter's *soul* (his conscious experience). In his human *spirit,* Jesus was Lord and had been ever since Peter responded to Jesus' call and entered into life.

It is quite possible then for you habitually to walk in the Spirit in one area of life—say, your relations with Christian brothers and sisters—but perhaps the moment you are involved with a member of your immediate family, you enter an area where the flesh is still unconquered and speech and attitudes are fleshly instead of Spirit-governed. This frequently happens with young Christians. From His vantage point in your human spirit the Spirit of God exerts steady and unyielding pressure upon the area of family relationships, often precipitating several crises, until the will submits in that area and Jesus is enthroned as Lord there too. Thus another degree of likeness to Christ is achieved and another degree of glory manifested.

Perhaps it is the sex life that holds out against the control of the Spirit. Or it may be the vocational life. Many a businessman has learned to live in the Spirit on Sundays, but on Monday morning when he steps across the threshold of his office, he says, in effect, "Here I am in control. I have been trained to handle affairs here, and I don't need God's help. I know what is expected of me and I can handle things on my own." That, of course, is the old covenant in its purest form, and such a procedure will guarantee the presence in that businessman of many forms of death: depression, boredom, resentment, anxiety, tension, and so on.

Fighting a battle already won

Since we can live only in one area of relationships of our life at any given moment, it is evident that we can be in a Spirit-controlled area one moment and in a flesh-dominated area the next. This is why we can be a great person to live with one minute (delightful, because we are in the Spirit) and then a moment later some old habit of the flesh reasserts itself and we are right back in our old covenant behavior—harsh, nasty, or cruel. When we become aware of those feelings within, we know we will lose our Christian reputation if they are allowed to show, so we snatch an evangelical veil and hide the fading glory.

But how encouraging to know that the Spirit will never give up the battle! He seeks in a thousand ways to invade each separate relationship of the soul, and gradually He is doing so—sometimes faster, as we yield to him; sometimes very slowly, as we resist and cling to our veils. The more we work and live with the face of Jesus clearly in view, the more quickly we find each area of our life being changed into His likeness. We cannot do that work. It is, as Paul says, all "from the Lord, who is the Spirit." He will never cease the work He has begun.

VII

The Enemy Without

IF YOU LOOK UP the biography of General John Sedgwick in an encyclopedia, it will tell you he was a Union officer who was killed in action at the Battle of the Wilderness in the Civil War. But it probably won't tell you how he died. Here is the story:

The general was walking along the wall of a fortification, inspecting his troops. He came to a notch in the protective parapet of the fort, where he paused for a moment to look out across the battlefield toward the enemy lines.

One of Sedgwick's officer's cleared his throat nervously. "General," he said, "I don't think it's safe to stand there. You are exposed to the enemy's muzzle."

"Nonsense," the general replied confidently. "They couldn't hit an elephant at this dist—"

And those were his last words. It doesn't pay to underestimate your enemy. In the spiritual realm, our enemy is Satan, and many Christians have made the fatal mistake of underestimating his deadly power. In this chapter, we take a closer look at our enemy so that we can better understand—and defend ourselves against—his strategy.

Our ministry

As we have already seen, on the basis of the new covenant, we can quickly handle *inner* problems—fear, tension, hostility, inadequacy, or shame—as we enthrone Jesus Christ in our lives and trust His love and care for us. In this way, we are left free to concentrate on the ministry before us—a ministry Paul refers to (with that eternal optimism that marked his apostolic career), when he says, "Since through God's mercy we have this ministry, we do not lose heart" (2 Corinthians 4:1). In the original Greek the word translated "this" is very definitive; "this kind of a ministry" is the thought. The kind he refers to is what he has just described: a ministry in the new covenant where all veils are removed by a continual turning to the Lord, and where the Spirit within reveals the character of Christ in ever-increasing areas of life.

How can there be room for discouragement in that kind of a ministry? There will be failures, for the flesh is wily and elusive, but they need only be momentary setbacks. In any case, God never intended our mistakes to produce condemnation in our lives. Rather, each mistake we make is to be a learning experience that leads to our growth, restoration, and renewed activity in the strength of the Lord. Because we have been given this ministry by a merciful God, we do not lose heart—even when we make mistakes. By God's mercy, we pick ourselves up and keep moving forward.

Whatever form our ministry takes, it will bear the characteristic marks of the new covenant—simplicity, liberty, and effectiveness. Paul describes it in these terms: "We have renounced secret and shameful ways; we do not use deception, nor do we distort the word of God. On the contrary, by setting forth the truth plainly we commend ourselves to every man's conscience in the sight of God" (2 Corinthians 4:2).

In line with the two-step walk in the Spirit we discussed in the previous chapter, we have here also a negative and positive description of a new covenant ministry. First, the negative: "We have renounced secret and shameful ways; we do not use deception, nor do we distort the word of God." Once again the first century sounds strangely like our own. In Paul's time there were men (and surely, women too) who considered it necessary to produce instant and visible results so they could appear successful in ministry. It didn't matter whether the ministry was a public or private one, success rested upon obtaining some visible sign of achievement. Consequently, they turned to what Paul calls "secret and shameful ways" to produce the desired results.

Similar activities of our own day suggest specifically what these disgraceful tactics were. Undoubtedly they consisted of psychological gimmicks, pressure tactics, emotional pleas, heavy-handed demands, just as we see all too frequently today. They would also include high-powered promotional campaigns, self-advertising posters and handouts, and the continual emphasis upon numbers as an indicator of success. There is, of course, a legitimate use of publicity for informational purposes, but promotion is something else again. Jesus warned, "Whoever exalts himself will be humbled, and whoever humbles himself will be exalted" (Matthew 23:12).

In straightforward fashion, Paul renounced all these psychological tricks to gain impressive results. Perhaps he had even practiced them himself in the days of his phariseeism, and even, for awhile, after he became a

Christian. But no more. A qualified minister of the new covenant did not need them. Furthermore, he refused to practice deception (or, as the RSV has it, "cunning"), as evidently many others were doing in his day. The thought behind *cunning* is a readiness to try anything. It conveys the idea of being unprincipled, without morals or scruples. In these days of religious racketeers, it hardly requires any enlarging upon. It is simple expediency, justifying the means by the apparently good ends achieved.

A final state of dishonesty was reached by those who descended to actually tampering with the Word of God to obtain the appearance of success they desired. This was not, as we might think today, an altering of the text of the Bible. Very few copies of the Scriptures were available in the first century. It meant, rather, a twisting of the meaning of Scripture or a misapplication of truth—a pressing of it to unwarranted extremes. A case in point is that of Hymeneas and Philetus who taught that the resurrection was already past (2 Timothy 2:17–18). While they didn't deny the resurrection, they tampered with the Word of God by relegating the resurrection to the past. It was probably a result of teaching partial truth instead of the entire scope of revelation. Many of the newer cults emerging today are employing this tactic to the confusion and hurt of many. True, this all sounds biblical, but it is actually tampering with the Word of God by subtle and devious means.

No boasting needed

None of these approaches is needed in a new covenant ministry, Paul declares. They mark the very antithesis of it, and the appearance of any of them in a ministry would indicate the indulgence of the flesh. There are a thousand or more ways by which the flesh can seek to counterfeit the work of the Spirit, and they are all aimed at one point: the achieving of an appearance of "success," which can then be used to enhance the prestige or status of the persons concerned. Because these practices are so prevalent in our day (as they evidently were in the first century, too) many young, relatively immature Christians are caught up in them without realizing it. Since few voices are raised to challenge them, such practices are easily accepted as proper. But it is at this point that the Word of God must judge us all. As Paul says a little later in this same letter, "'Let him who boasts boast in the Lord.' For it is not the one who commends himself who is approved, but the one whom the Lord commends" (2 Corinthians 10:17–18).

In stark contrast to the multiplicity of evil is the simplicity of truth. In a great positive declaration, the apostle describes his own practice and the practice of all who labor in the liberty and sweetness of the new covenant: "by setting forth the truth plainly we commend ourselves to every man's conscience in the sight of God" (2 Corinthians 4:2b).

A precise and clear definition of a new covenant ministry as it would appear in any public manifestation is single and invariable: "by setting forth the truth plainly." Nothing more is ever needed. The truth as it is in Jesus is so radical, so startling in its breadth of dimension, so universal, so relevant to human life everywhere that no psychological tricks are needed to prop it up and make it effective or interesting. It is the most captivating subject known, for it concerns man himself, and at his deepest levels.

Right before God

The goal of Paul's proclamation is equally clear: "we commend ourselves to every man's conscience." The conscience, as used here, is the will of the human spirit as contrasted to that more fluctuating and flexible entity, the will of the soul. It is what a man knows he "ought" to do, whether he always does it or not. It is the deep awareness within every person of what it takes to be the kind of person he or she admires and basically wants to be.

To appeal to the conscience, therefore, is to seek to capture the whole man: body, soul, and spirit—mentally, emotionally, and volitionally. It does not aim at mere intellectual agreement and certainly not at a shallow emotional commitment. Rather, it seeks to impress the conscience that commitment to Jesus is right; that is, in line with reality, and the only way to true fulfillment. It does not, therefore, demand immediate and visible results, though it will welcome any that may come; it is content to allow time for the growth of the seed that is planted and recognizes that individuals can properly respond only to what they clearly understand.

Finally, this is to be done "in the sight of God." As we have seen, this means an awareness that God is watching all that is done, appraising it and seeking to correct it where needed. But the phrase suggests even more. Since the new covenant is "everything coming from God," it means also that the inner eye of the soul is looking to God for the supply of power and resource to make the ministry effective. The responsibility for results is placed squarely on God alone. This is what gives the spirit of the worker a sense of serenity and peace. He or she is free to be an instrument in God's hands. That is the new covenant ministry in its outreach to the world.

That veil again

At this point in Paul's letter the unpleasant realities of life intrude again. That is the glory of the gospel; it never deals merely with the ideal but with life as it truly is. Ideally, if God is responsible for results and is desirous that all men be saved, then whenever the gospel is preached or taught there should be many responses. But in actual practice, this is not always true. What about those times? To this implied question the apostle responds: "Even if our gospel is veiled, it is veiled to those who are perishing. The god of this age has blinded the minds of unbelievers, so that they cannot see the light of the gospel of the glory of Christ, who is the image of God" (2 Corinthians 4:3–4).

Once again the veil of pride appears in this discussion. The reference this time is not to the veils evangelicals employ but to those used by worldly men and women when they are confronted with the good news about Jesus. Paul referred earlier to the phenomenon of being at the same time "life unto life" to some who hear his preaching and "death unto death" to others. The latter fail to see anything good in the "good news" because a veil covers their minds, obscuring their ability to perceive the truth. To them the gospel appears unrealistic, remote from real life, making its appeal only to those who have a streak of "religion" in them. But it is their outlook that is the illusion.

And here is where we glimpse the enemy without. As Paul puts it, "The god of this age [Satan] has blinded the minds of unbelievers." As always, Satan uses pride to blind their eyes. They are so confident of their own ability to handle life, so sure that they have what it takes to solve their problems. To them, therefore, Jesus appears to be dispensable, hardly worth considering. They fail to see that He stands at the center of life and that all reality derives its content from him. To argue against Him is to argue with the very power that makes it possible to take the breath that voices the argument! Jesus is Lord, whether men know it or not, and ultimately "at the name of Jesus every knee should bow, in heaven and on earth and under the earth, and every tongue confess that Jesus Christ is Lord, to the glory of God the Father" (Philippians 2:10–11).

Don't dodge life—or death

It is helpful to know just when this satanic blinding takes place. A superficial reading of the passage leaves the impression that the minds are blinded or veiled after they hear the gospel preached. They hear it and reject it and, as a consequence, their minds are blinded. That is the common way of understanding this passage. But Paul declares that the blinding is to keep people from seeing the light of the gospel, therefore it must occur *before* the gospel is heard. They are called "unbelievers," not because they don't believe the gospel, but because there is something else they have not believed in even before the gospel was heard. What is that? It is *reality*, the way things really are. The god of this world, the enemy without, has successfully accustomed them to live by illusions which they take to be reality. They are not willing to face life as it is. Men are turned away from truth long before they hear the gospel because they *refuse to examine life realistically.*

A common example of this is the way many people avoid the word *death*. Death is an unpleasant subject, yet it is a stark reality with which every one of us must ultimately wrestle. Watch how uncomfortable many people are at funerals and how they want the service to be as short as possible in order to return to the familiar illusions they regard as real. Instead of grappling with the fact of death and facing its implications in life right now (which might very well prepare them to believe the gospel when they hear it), they choose to run away and hide their heads in the sand until the inevitable encounter with death leaves them no way of escape.

Escapism can be seen in many other ways, as well. Most people do not like to see themselves as they really are. They choose to believe a more acceptable image of themselves, even though moments of truth may come when they suddenly see themselves unveiled. Some people train themselves to avoid anything unpleasant or difficult, and so they find themselves unwittingly trapped by the god of this world into believing fantasies and treating illusions as though they were real. Such people are very difficult to reach with the gospel. To them it is often a fragrance of death unto death.

Yet, occasionally, one meets non-Christians who have been trained to face life realistically and not to run from difficult things. They are usually those who have had a considerable amount of self-discipline and are accustomed to taking orders from someone else. For example, soldiers frequently fit this description. Upon hearing the gospel they often accept it immediately. To them Jesus "fits." They sense immediately that He is that missing center they have long been seeking. Their eyes are not veiled.

The secret of being like God

It is tragic, though, that those who fail to see the gospel as reality are turning away from the very thing they most desperately want to find. The center of the gospel is Christ, and Christ, as Paul tells us here, is the likeness of God. Therefore, what is lost to these people is the secret of godlikeness—and that is what men long for more than anything else. God is a totally independent being, having no need within Himself for anyone or anything else, and yet, in love, giving

The Enemy Without 113

Himself freely to all His creatures. It is that same kind of independence which humanity craves. To most people, that is the essence of godlikeness, and that is why people are clamoring, "Let me be myself! I've gotta be me!"

What people fail to understand, in this veiled view of reality, is that such independence for human beings must arise out of dependence. God wants people to be godlike. He wants us to be independent of all other creatures or things in the universe precisely because we are totally dependent on Him.

It was no lie for Satan to say to Eve in the garden, "When you eat of [this fruit] . . . you will be like God." It was very difficult for Eve to see anything wrong with that because, after all, that was what God wanted. He desires godlike people. This is apparent throughout Scripture. "What is man that you are mindful of him, the son of man that you care for him? You made him a little lower than the heavenly beings and crowned him with glory and honor" (Psalm 8:4–5). What Eve did not understand was that only through Christ is godlikeness possible. Paul expresses his own amazement over the concept in 1 Timothy 3:16, "Beyond all question, the mystery of godliness is great: He appeared in a body . . . ." Godlikeness is, of course, the new covenant in action— "everything coming from God, nothing coming from me."

The light dawns

Well, what about these people whose minds are blinded? Are they without hope? Is there no way to reach them in their darkness? Paul's answer to that is magnificent: "We do not preach ourselves, but Jesus Christ as Lord, and ourselves as your servants for Jesus' sake. For God, who said, 'Let light shine out of darkness,' made his light shine in our hearts to give us the light of the knowledge of the glory of God in the face of Christ" (2 Corinthians 4:5–6).

Paul's argument is that the preaching of Jesus as Lord (the center and heart of all reality, the one in control of all events) is a message that is honored by God, and God is a being of incredible power and authority. In fact, He is the one who at creation commanded the light to *shine out* of darkness. Notice, He did not command the light to shine *into* the darkness—He literally commanded the darkness to produce light!

Now why are these people perishing? Their minds, Paul said, are blinded; that is, they live in darkness. They have already turned from the normal way by which God proposes to save people—that is, by an honest response to reality (see Hebrews 11:6). But their case is not hopeless, for the God whom Paul preaches is able to call light out of darkness. Light they must have, but if they reject the light of nature and life, there is still the possibility that when they hear the good news that Jesus is Lord, God will do a creative act and call light *out of* their Stygian darkness. For this reason the Christian can always witness in hope, knowing that a sovereign God will work in resurrection power to call light out of darkness in many hearts. Jesus knew this: "All that the Father gives me will come to me, and whoever comes to me I will never drive away" (John 6:37).

Paul sees himself as one of these men. Before his conversion experience he had been intent on pleasing God, committed to this great objective and doing his dedicated best to fulfill it, yet the darkness in which he lived was so deep that when he saw and heard Jesus, he could not recognize Him as the Son of God but thought

Him to be a usurper and a vagabond. But on the road to Damascus Paul was suddenly overwhelmed with light. Out of the darkness of his brilliant mind the light shone and illuminated the darkness of his dedicated heart. There he experienced what he had long sought—the knowledge of the glory of God. To his utter amazement he found it where he least expected: in the face of Jesus Christ.

God set aside young Saul's brilliance, his dedication, and his blameless morality as having done nothing to advance him on his search for reality. Suddenly it was all made clear—Jesus is Lord! Using that key, everything began to fall into place; the universe and life itself began to make sense. And best of all, Paul found himself fulfilled as a man. Jesus was real and was with him night and day. Courage and peace and power were his as a daily inheritance, enriching his life beyond all expectation. He had found the secret of godlikeness—of *being like God!*

Because of his own experience the apostle is careful now to keep his preaching sharply focused on the only subject God will honor by calling light out of darkness—that is, "We do not preach ourselves, but Jesus Christ as Lord, and ourselves as your servants for Jesus' sake" (2 Corinthians 4:5). The danger in preaching is that all too often we offer ourselves as the remedy for man's need. We speak about the church or Christian education or the Christian way of life, when all the time what people need is Jesus. The church cannot save, a knowledge of Christian philosophy does not heal, doctrine without love puffs up. Only Jesus is Lord, only He is absolutely essential to life. When one encounters Him, all the other things will fall into their proper places.

A servant heart

In view of this, the role of the Christian is that of a servant. He is there to discover the needs of others and to do whatever his master tells him to do to meet those needs. He is, therefore, a servant "for Jesus' sake." He is never the servant of men, but he is Jesus' servant and therefore serves men. That is an important distinction. A friend of mine said, "The tragic error I made was that I became a servant of people. I felt obligated to respond favorably when anyone called and asked me to do something. Someone would say, 'I think you ought to do such and such,' and I would say, 'Right, I'd better do it.' Then five other people would tell me what they thought I should do. Suddenly I found myself in trouble because I couldn't do everything. But when I checked the life of Jesus, I found that He was a servant of the Father, not a servant of people. He submitted Himself to the people whom the Father picked out. That set me free."

God always honors a message centered on the lordship of Jesus, and that manifests a servant's heart to those He sets in your path. The god of this world, the enemy without, is clever and subtle. He knows how to lead men into darkness without their being aware of what is happening. But the God of resurrection is more than his equal. He will honor the open statement of the truth with the light of the glory of God, pouring from the face of Jesus Christ.

Pots, Pressures, and Power

What is light?

Scientists tell us that until light is received by the eye and interpreted by the brain, it is just electro-magnetic radiation. The universe is flooded with electromagnetic radiation, most of it invisible to the human eye. Gamma rays, X-rays, microwaves, radio waves, infrared waves, ultraviolet waves, cosmic waves—these are all forms of electromagnetic radiation that are invisible to us. Only a very narrow portion of the vast electromagnetic spectrum is visible to the human eye—the portion we see in a rainbow or in the rainbow-like spectrum of color that comes from a prism.

Yet God has designed our eyes and our brains in such a way that they can transform that narrow range of electromagnetic radiation into information, meaning, and emotion. That's right, emotion! We human beings perceive colors as *emotional qualities.* To us, red is a "warm" and "exciting" color, blue is "cool" and "serene." A field of wildflowers can fill us with a joy so intense, it verges on grief.

Our ability to experience the many shades of light and color as shades of meaning and emotion is an echo, a reflection of the appreciative capacity of God our Creator. He looked upon the light that streamed from the stars and galaxies He had created, the light that sparkled on the oceans and snow-capped peaks He had arranged, the light that fell through the leaves of the forests brimming with life. He saw the light that highlighted the beautifully molded features of the people He had made in his own image—and He declared it all "good."

Light is one of the most powerful and meaningful of all the visual symbols God uses to illustrate spiritual reality in His Word. The miracle of regeneration has been described by the apostle Paul as light, springing up suddenly from midnight darkness. Light makes no noise and cannot be touched or felt, but it is unmistakable. It not only can be seen, but it is the medium by which we see everything else. "That is what coming to Christ is like," Paul says, in effect. "It enlightens you by the knowledge of the glory of God."

But Christianity is more than conversion. It is, as we have seen, a *total life* to be lived in the midst of this present world without evasion or defeat. It is opposed by the flesh within and the devil without so that one thing is certain—it won't be easy! But though total life isn't easy, it will be remarkable, as Paul makes clear in his description of the authentic Christian life beyond conversion: "We have this treasure in jars of clay to show that this all-surpassing power is from God and not from us" (2 Corinthians 4:7).

Nothing but pots

Note two profoundly important factors in this verse: the description of basic humanity and the revelation of the intent of God. Paul first looks at the basic material with which God works, and he describes it as a lowly vessel—"We have this treasure in jars of clay." This is not the only place in Scripture where this expression occurs. Perhaps you have never thought of yourself as a vessel, but it is a fundamental and essential aspect of the biblical view of humanity.

What are vessels for? They are essentially containers made to hold something. The vessels in your home (pots, cups, bowls) are made to contain something, and when nothing is in them they are, of course, empty vessels. That is the significance of this verse of Scripture. It reminds us that we human beings were intended to contain something.

What were we made to contain? This alluring question has set humanity on a quest for his own identity since time began. The startling answer of the Bible is that we are made to contain God! The glory of our humanity is that it was intended to hold the Almighty. Our humanity is designed to correspond to deity. "Now the dwelling of God is with men, and he will live with them. They will be his people, and God himself will be with them and be their God. He will wipe every tear from their eyes" (Revelation 21:3–4). That is the glory of humanity.

It is accurate to describe lives without God as "empty lives." That is exactly what they are—devoid of what they were meant to contain. Dr. Carl Jung has described the world today as suffering from "a neurosis of emptiness." The result is hollow men and women who display an outward shell of busyness and interest but inwardly they are nothing but an echoing emptiness.

It is fascinating to discover that in this verse we are not just vessels, but we are (as the King James Version puts it) "earthen vessels"—made from clay, very common material, which in itself has little value. There is nothing very impressive about human beings in and of themselves. Despite our vast God-given possibilities and our specious claim to great wisdom and cleverness, we must face the humbling fact that we are directly responsible for the terrible problems that now throttle the earth. Apart from God, we are nothing but humble earthen pots—and sometimes we are *cracked* pots at that!

Of course, there are all kinds and grades of clay. Some people are like fine china—they crack easily. While they have a very fine texture, it is nothing more than a form of clay. Others are more like sun-dried mud and crumble at the first rap. Some are tough and resilient by nature, and others are pliable and easily molded. But all are clay. Underneath, we are all ordinary people.

Hidden treasure

But the Christian is more than an empty vessel. He has something within—or, more accurately, *Someone* within. We have a treasure in our clay pot! And more than a treasure—a transcendent power! That is humanity as God intended it to be. The clay pot is not much in itself, but it holds an inestimable treasure, beyond price, and a transcendent power, greater than any other power known to humanity.

That is the second great truth found in this verse of Scripture. God has designed even ordinary people like us so that we may be the bearers of the most remarkable riches and power ever known. It must be apparent to all, however, that the treasure and the power are not from us, but from God. Does that not sound familiar? "Nothing coming from us; everything coming from God." The point is that God designed it this way; He intended that His great power, wisdom, and love should become visible in very ordinary and otherwise inconsequential people. As Paul observes in 1 Corinthians 1:27–29, "God chose the foolish things of the world to shame the wise; God chose the weak things of the world to shame the strong. He chose the lowly things of this world and the despised things— and the things that are not—to nullify the things that are, so that no one may boast before him."

The tremendous thing about all this is that the apostle is not merely using beautiful imagery. He is speaking of hard realities, of something genuine and practical, not merely idealistic and visionary. Each believer contains an inestimable treasure, a power beyond all telling. Paul puts it in clear terms to the Colossians as he describes his ministry to them: "To them [the apostles] God has chosen to make known among the Gentiles *the glorious riches of this mystery,* which is *Christ in you,* the hope of glory" (Colossians 1:27, emphasis added).

The only hope we have of realizing, even in this present life, the glory God intended for us is to learn to draw upon the treasure within and be empowered by the power available. That treasure and that power are Christ, in you! So valuable is the treasure that the world would pay anything to get it. It is, as we have seen, the secret of human adequacy, and billions of dollars are poured out every week in a vain effort to identify this treasure and channel it into the normal affairs of life.

"Christ in you" is the lost secret of humanity, but when the full implications of the secret are realized, a person's life is enriched far beyond the ability to declare it. That is what sent Paul around the world of his day declaring what he called "the unsearchable riches of Christ." To see lonely, selfish, empty individuals transformed slowly but surely into warm, loving, wholesome, and happy people is to become aware of why Paul describes Christ as "unsearchable riches."

The great secret within is such a treasure because, first of all, it is a transcendent power. *Transcendent* means beyond the ordinary. It is a completely different form of power. So often, in our time, power is used to tear things apart, to blast, or explode, or crush. But transcendent power unites, gathers, harmonizes. It breaks down walls of partition and removes barriers. It does not make superficial, external adjustments, but works from within, producing permanent trans-formations. Do you know of any other power like that? It is absolutely unrivaled; like nothing else. Many philosophies and teachings seek to imitate this, and for a time they may produce a credible likeness, but in the end they all prove to be cheap and shoddy imitations. They cannot stand the tests to which life as it really is will expose them. In the end only "Christ in you" endures.

By design God entrusts this secret to failing, faulty, weak, and sinful people so it will be clear that the power does not originate with us. It isn't the result of a strong personality or of a keen and finely honed mind or of good breeding and training. No, it arises solely from the presence of God in the heart. Our earthiness must be as apparent to others as the power is, so that they may see that the secret is not us but God. That is why we must be transparent people, not hiding our weaknesses and failures, but honestly admitting them when they occur.

Headed for trouble

To show how immensely practical these biblical truths are, the apostle goes on to describe the way it works in the trenches of daily living: "We are hard pressed on every side, but not crushed; perplexed, but not in despair; persecuted, but not abandoned; struck down, but not destroyed" (2 Corinthians 4:8–9).

All the pressures common to humanity are present in the life of a Christian. Undoubtedly, one of the greatest misconceptions held by many is that being a Christian means that life should suddenly smooth out, mysterious bridges will appear over all chasms, the winds of fate will be tempered, and all difficulties will disappear. No, Christianity is not membership in some red-carpet club. All the problems and pressures of life remain, or are even intensified. Christians must face life in the raw, just as any pagan will. The purpose of the Christian life is not to escape dangers and difficulties but to demonstrate a different way of handling them. There must be trouble, or there can be no demonstration. Look at the four categories of trouble Paul describes:

1. *Afflictions:* "We are pressed on every side." These are the normal irritations of life which everyone faces—the bothersome, troublesome incidents that afflict us. The washing machine breaks down on Monday morning; it rains on your day off; the dog gets sick on the new carpet; your mother-in-law arrives unexpectedly for a long visit; the traffic is worse than usual; you flunk the exam you expected to pass. All these are normal afflictions. They are the buffetings of life that everyone experiences. Christians are not exempted from them.

2. *Perplexities:* Even the apostles did not always know what to do. They were sometimes uncertain and couldn't understand why God allowed some things to

happen in their lives. They occasionally found it difficult to make decisions, just like the rest of us. Paul said he tried to go into Bithynia, but the Spirit would not allow him to do so. He intended to preach the gospel in the province of Asia, but was ultimately forbidden by the Holy Spirit (see Acts 16). Even Jesus seems to fluctuate, telling His brothers He is not going up to the Feast of Tabernacles, and later changing His mind and going (see John 7). There will be many times of uncertainty in our lives, many occasions when we do not understand what to do, what to say, or why things happen the way they do. These are normal perplexities.

3. *Persecutions:* The Christian is promised persecutions. Even the "worldlings"—those who are in and of this dying world—are often persecuted, but the Christian can absolutely count on it and expect it, for his Master was persecuted also. The word *persecution* covers the entire range of deliberate offenses against Christians from slight ostracisms, cold shoulders, and critical remarks to smears on reputations, hindrances to ministry, personal and bodily attacks, and even torture and death. Christians can expect any or all of these. The apostles were persecuted unto death, as even the Lord was, and "no servant is greater than his master."

4. *Catastrophes:* "Struck down!" This phrase has power to chill the heart. It refers to the stunning, shattering blows that seem to come to us out of the blue—cancer, fatal accidents, a heart attack, riot, war, earthquakes, Alzheimer's disease, insanity. Christians are not always protected from these catastrophic events. They are terrible experiences that severly try our faith and leave us frightened and baffled. The book of Job is clear proof that these stunning catastrophes can happen to believers and that the loving heart of God is nevertheless behind them.

Authentic Christians—and unbelieving believers

But look at the reactions to these trials Paul describes. "We are hard pressed on every side, *but not crushed*. Perplexed, *but not in despair*. Persecuted, *but not abandoned*. Struck down, *but not destroyed*" (emphasis added). There is a power within, a transcendent power, different from anything else, that keeps pushing back with greater pressure against whatever comes from without, so that we are not crushed, despairing, forsaken, or destroyed.

This power within was given to us for the very purpose of handling life's afflictions. We are exposed to them so that we might demonstrate a different reaction than one that would come from a person of the world. Our neighbors, watching us, will find us difficult to explain, and it is only when we baffle them that we are likely to impress them with the advantage our faith gives. There will be a quality about us that can be explained only in terms of God at work. It must be evident that the power belongs to God and not to us.

When we ask ourselves whether this actually *is* the reaction of Christians to the normal trials of life, we must hang our heads in shame. All too often we react exactly as the unbelievers around us—and sometimes not as well. We lose our tempers at minor irritations, we grow pouty and sulky when we're not given the favored place, we resent the perplexities to which we are exposed, and grow bitter and sullen at the catastrophes we experience.

In all this we reveal ourselves as unbelieving believers. Our problem is, as we have seen before, that we are either ignorant of the way of escape or do not choose to use it because we desire to have *both* the pleasure of sin *and* the deliverance that comes from the transcendent power within.

But this is not possible. No one can serve two masters.

Once again the apostle brings us the key. In a passage of infinite light and beauty he indicates the process of switching from the old covenant, with its built-in death, to the new covenant and its power and life. The process requires a certain invariable order: "We always carry around in our body the death of Jesus, so that the life of Jesus may also be revealed in our body. For we who are alive are always being given over to death for Jesus' sake, so that his life may be revealed in our mortal body" (2 Corinthians 4:10–11).

The life of Jesus, manifest in our mortal bodies, right now, in time, is what we need and want. Two factors can produce it. One is an inner attitude to which we must consent (verse 10). The other is an outward circumstance into which we are placed (verse 11). But the result is the same for each: the life of Jesus, manifest in our mortal flesh. Not in our immortal flesh, someday in heaven, but *right now,* precisely when we need it, when we are under the gun, facing the afflictions, perplexities, persecutions, and catastrophes of life!

What is the secret? It is, first, that we "always carry around in our body the death of Jesus." That is the inner attitude to which we must consent. The key to experiencing the life of Jesus is our willingness to accept the implications of His death. We will not discover the glory of the treasure and power within us until we are ready to accept in practical terms the result of the sacrificial, obedient death of Jesus.

The cross at work

The death of Jesus was by means of the cross, and the cross was designed for only one purpose: to end the existence of an evil man! Those who were crucified had no life in this world beyond that point. It may sound strange to us to apply the term "an evil man" to Jesus, but it must be remembered that a little further on in this very letter the apostle says, "God made him who had no sin to be sin for us, so that in him we might become the righteousness of God" (2 Corinthians 5:21). Literally, he was *made sin.* He became what we are. When He became what we are (evil men), there was nothing God could do except to put Him to death. That is what God does with evil people; He puts them to death. Thus, in the cross of Christ, God took all that we are in Adam, all our natural life with its dreams and hopes and resources and brought it to a crashing end by Jesus' death.

The cross of Jesus put to death the proud ego within us. It wrote off as utterly worthless the faculty within us that wants to blow a trumpet whenever we do what we think is good. It sentences to death that inner desire that wants no one else to be as educated or as popular or as skillful or as beautiful as we. It is the thing within us that struggles to be at the center at all times and expresses itself in self-pity, self-indulgence, self-excuse, and self-assertion.

I must clearly understand that it is not up to me to put this natural life to death—*it has already been done.* I am only expected to agree with the rightness of that execution and stop trying to make it "live" again before God. When a son was promised to Abraham, he cried to God, "If only Ishmael might live under your blessing!" (Genesis 17:18). But God refused, for Isaac was the child of promise, not Ishmael. Abraham must learn that though Ishmael was permitted to exist, God would fulfill none of His promise of blessing through him. Only through Isaac would the blessing come.

Thus when I cease trying to justify and excuse the activities of the flesh and agree with God that the flesh is rightfully under sentence of death, then I am fulfilling this powerful figure of always carrying around in my body the death of Jesus. If I welcome the cross and see that it has already put to death the flesh rising within me so that it can have no power over me, then I find myself able to say no to its cry for expression. I can then turn instead to the Lord Jesus with the full expectation that as I will to do what He tells me to do in these circumstances (love my enemies, flee youthful lusts, wait patiently for the Lord, and so forth), He will be at work in me to enable me to do it. Thus the life of Jesus will be manifest in my mortal life.

This necessity to agree with the implications of the cross in terms of actual experience is what Jesus has in mind when He says, "If anyone would come after me, he must deny himself and take up his cross and follow me" (Mark 8:34). Paul is saying exactly the same thing here. The key to the new life is the belief that the old has been rendered of no value whatsoever by the cross. And throughout Scripture the order never varies. First death, then life. Death is intended to lead to resurrection. "If we died with him, we will also live with him" (2 Timothy 2:11). When we consent to death, then the life of Jesus can flow unhindered from us. It is never the other way. We cannot claim resurrection life first, and then by means of that put the flesh to death. We must first bow to the cross, then God will bring about the resurrection.

Something done to us

The second factor that produces the life of Jesus in us is: "We who are alive are always being given over to death for Jesus' sake, so that his life may be revealed in our mortal body" (2 Corinthians 4:11). That sounds very much like the first, but there is an important difference.

The first was an attitude within to which we must consent. It was stated in the active voice (always carrying in the body the death of Jesus). The second is stated in the passive voice, that is, it is something done to us, not something we are to do. We have no choice in this second matter. We are being given up to death. This refers to those circumstances of trial and pressure into which God puts us to force us to abandon trust in the flesh and lean wholly on the Spirit of Christ.

The encouraging thing about this is to see that it is impossible for a true believer in Jesus not to walk in the Spirit at least some of the time. God will see to it that the true believer is put in circumstances that force the issue. A case in point is the experience of Peter walking on the water. When he first got out of the boat and walked on the water to Jesus, it was by his own choice, though the power to do so came from the Lord. However when Peter's gaze wandered and he began to sink, it was a moment of desperation. It was either look to Christ or perish. When he cried out in terror, "Lord, save me!" Jesus lifted him up and they walked back to the boat together. So God is forever putting us into situations where we are way over our depth and are forced to abandon hope in all human resources and cry out, "Lord, save me!" Paul calls this being "given over to death for Jesus' sake."

Paul uses his own experience as a perfect illustration. "We do not want you to be uninformed, brothers, about the hardships we suffered in the province of Asia. We were under great pressure, far beyond our ability to endure, so that we despaired even of life. Indeed, in our hearts we felt the sentence of death. But this happened that we might not rely on ourselves but on God, who raises the dead" (2 Corinthians 1:8–9).

We do not know which experience Paul is describing here. Perhaps it was the riot that broke out in Ephesus as recorded in Acts 19. At any rate it was something so threatening and so dangerous that Paul despaired of life itself. He felt he had received the sentence of death. He was, literally, "being given over to death for Jesus' sake." Notice, though, Paul's conclusion: "But this happened that we might not rely on ourselves but on God, who raises the dead."

God put Paul through this trying circumstance to keep him from relying on his own resources. And this is said of an apostle who thoroughly knew and understood the new covenant. Even he needed this painful help from time to time to keep him from succumbing to the subtlety of the flesh and to enable him to trust the God who raises the dead, the God of resurrection power.

This is why pressures and problems arise in our lives. The God who loves us is delivering us up to death in order that we might trust, not in happy circumstances or in pleasant surroundings, but in the Lord of life who lives within. In the Scriptures we learn the attitude we are to have that releases to us the life of Jesus. Through our circumstances we are forced to *experience* this so that the treasure within might enrich us and the power within demonstrate before a watching world a totally new and different way of life.

Walking through life

Here we see a powerful, life-changing, two-step process—a process that is repeated throughout Scripture, a process it describes as "walking in the Spirit." We are to believe in the death of the cross and then appropriate the power of the resurrection. The simplest way to put it is: repent and believe. *Repenting* is changing one's mind about the value of the old life; *believing* is appropriating the value of the new. In Romans 6 Paul says, "Count yourselves dead to sin" (step one) "but alive to God in Christ Jesus" (step two). In Ephesians he says, "Put off your old self" (step one), and "put on the new" (step two). These are not widely differing things; they are the same, but stated in different ways so that all will understand. A walk consists of two steps, one with each leg, repeated again and again. So the walk in the Spirit is achieved when we meet every demand life makes on us by taking up the cross, so that we might experience the resurrection. It can happen dozens of times a day.

All this has an effect far beyond one individual life. The apostle says to the Corinthians:

> So then, death is at work in us, but life is at work in you. It is written: "I believed; therefore I have spoken." With that same spirit of faith we also believe and therefore speak, because we know that the one who raised the Lord Jesus from the dead will also raise us with Jesus and present us with you in his presence. All this is for your benefit, so that the grace that is reaching more and more people may cause thanksgiving to overflow to the glory of God (2 Corinthians 4:12–15).

This passage is a recognition that the glorious effects of the life of Jesus may not always be fully seen in a single believer's life. Sometimes the death is felt by one, and the resulting life by another. Paul feels this is the case with him. "Death is at work in us, but life is at work in you." The Corinthians were experiencing the benefit of the death to which Paul was daily being delivered. He was content with this, being willing to be sacrificed for their faith so that they might understand and grow in the grace of Christ. His quotation is from Psalm 116:10 where the writer speaks of being sorely afflicted and not knowing quite why, but he had nevertheless believed in God and so had spoken of deliverance even before it came, saying, "For you, O LORD, have delivered my soul from death, my eyes from tears, my feet from stumbling" (Psalm 116:8). Thus Paul, too, is confident that God will strengthen him along with the Corinthians and bring them all together into the fullness of glory.

The closing sentence in the passage above is a magnificent statement of the unity of believers as members of one another. What affects one affects all. But though there are suffering, death, and tears, yet it is all working together for good, and as the new covenant is understood by more and more believers, it will result in a great outburst of praise and thanksgiving to the glory of God. Who can help but praise a God who can bring joy out of sorrow, life out of death, and liberty out of bondage? This is the new way of life that the church is called upon to demonstrate before a watching world.

But even that is not the whole story. This present experience only points the way to something beyond, which is so breathtaking, so glorious, that the apostle is at a loss for adequate words to describe it. That is the adventure that awaits us in the next chapter.

Time and Eternity

EVER SINCE THE PUBLICATION of H.G. Wells' The Time Machine in 1895, people have been captivated by the idea of traveling in time. In that book, a scientist builds a time machine, travels far into the future, then returns and tells his astonished friends what the world will be like in 800,000 years! What most people fail to realize is that we don't need a machine to travel through time. The truth is, we are all time travelers. We are all traveling toward the future at a rate of one second per second, and we can do nothing to stop ourselves from time traveling.

And at the end of our journey through time is a destination we can scarcely imagine—a destination called eternity.

Everything in Scripture points to eternity, and everything within us cries out for it. As Solomon observed in the Old Testament, God "has also set eternity in the hearts of men; yet they cannot fathom what God has done from beginning to end" (Ecclesiastes 3:11). God designed us to live in eternity. His work with us is not finished in this life.

We have already seen that authentic Christianity is far more than a "pie in the sky, by and by" religion. It is magnificently designed for life on earth, right now, with all its pressures and problems, its joys and tears. But there is yet more for us to experience. God has prepared something incomprehensibly beautiful for those who love Him and trust Him—something that lies beyond time, something so beautiful and vast and breathtaking that only eternity is big enough to contain it. The apostle Paul tells us about the wonders of eternity in 2 Corinthians 4:16–18—and his description of eternity gives us grounds for confidence and courage as we face the trials and pressures of the present time:

> Therefore we do not lose heart. Though outwardly we are wasting away, yet inwardly we are being renewed day by day. For our light and momentary troubles are achieving for us an eternal glory that far outweighs them all. So we fix our eyes not on what is seen, but on what is unseen. For what is seen is temporary, but what is unseen is eternal.

Paul states plainly that what we are going through now is only preparing us for something yet to come—something so glorious and so different from what we have known that it is beyond all comparison. In the words of Robert Browning's "Rabbi Ben Ezra"—yet in a way far more true than Browning ever intended—Paul is saying:

> Grow old along with me!
> The best is yet to be,
> The last of life,
> for which the first was made.

This is the Christian hope. It is more than merely looking on to life beyond the grave. It declares that everything that happens to us in this life is directly related to what is coming—in fact, is getting us ready for it. Nothing, then, is purposeless or futile in our present experience. It is all necessary to the ultimate end.

The increasing beauty within

The apostle suggests three aspects of the Christian life indicate that something much greater is coming. First, there is the daily inner renewal. "Though outwardly we are wasting away," Paul says in 2 Corinthians 4:16, "yet inwardly we are being renewed day by day." The sharp contrast he draws is between the effects of aging upon the body—particularly our lessening physical power and approaching death—and the increase of wisdom and the mellowing of love that mark the spirit of one who walks with God. There is a beauty about godly old age of which youth knows nothing. The spirit broadens and grows serene though the body trembles and feels increasing pain.

What is happening? The outer man is losing the battle; the strength of youth falters and fades, the night is coming on. But the inner man is reaching out to light, growing in strength and beauty; the day is at hand. This inner renewal is another way of describing the new covenant in action. "Everything coming from God, nothing from me." The law of sin and death is destroying the body; the law of the Spirit of life in Christ Jesus is renewing the spirit and also the soul "with ever-increasing glory." To see this happening in oneself or in another is to be convinced that something wonderful lies ahead.

The authentic Christian view of trials

Furthermore, the apostle stoutly declares that our trials and hardships actually produce the glory to come! "For our light and momentary troubles are achieving for us an eternal glory that far outweighs them all" (2 Corinthians 4:17). Surely there is a twinkle in Paul's eye when he writes, "our light and momentary troubles," in view of what he at a later time describes.

> Five times I received from the Jews the forty lashes minus one. Three times I was beaten with rods, once I was stoned, three times I was shipwrecked, I spent a night and a day in the open sea, I have been constantly on the move. I have been in danger from rivers, in danger from bandits, in danger from my own countrymen, in danger from Gentiles; in danger in the city, in danger in the country, in danger at sea; and in danger from false brothers. I have labored and toiled and have often gone without sleep; I have known hunger and thirst and have often gone without food; I have been cold and naked (2 Corinthians 11:24–27).

That is what Paul calls "our light and momentary troubles." But he was not complaining. He made light of it simply because he was aware of something we often forget. He knew that these painful trials were actually preparing the "eternal glory that far outweighs them all." Notice he does not say that these trials were preparing him for the glory. While that was true, it wasn't what he said here. The trials were creating the glory!

Perhaps this throws some light on a strange statement Jesus made to His disciples in the Upper

Room. In saying that He was going away, He added, "I go to prepare a place for you" (John 14:2, KJV). This cryptic statement seems to suggest that heaven was not yet ready and needed some additional work before any guests arrived! But if we link it with the further explanation which Jesus gave them ("but if I go, I will send him [the Holy Spirit] to you," John 16:7), we have the strong suggestion that His way of preparing a place for them was to send the Holy Spirit to them. The Spirit, when He came, would give them the power to handle the pressures and pains of life ("hard pressed on every side, but not crushed; . . . struck down, but not destroyed") and in the mystery of redemption, transmute each trial into a corresponding glory. Thus, the trials were preparing the glory; the hardships were preparing "the place" for them. Jesus was doing it by means of the Spirit.

Valuable chains

A moving story comes out of the persecution of the Christians in the third and fourth centuries. One aged saint had spent many years in a dark and gloomy dungeon, bound by a great ball and chain. When the emperor Constantine ascended the throne, thousands of Christians were released from imprisonment, and among them this old man. Desiring to recompense him for his years of misery, the emperor commanded that the ball and chain be weighed and the old man given the equivalent weight in gold. Thus, the greater the weight of his chain, the greater was his reward when release came.

But the reality Paul speaks of is even greater than this. He says the weight of glory will be beyond all comparison. The Greek expression is, literally, "abundance upon abundance." It is such an abundance that it constitutes a great "weight." We speak of the "weight of responsibility" not always as a burden but often as a challenge. Here is the great challenge of a weight of glory, offering indescribable opportunity to those for whom it is prepared.

It seems clear, then, that something tremendous is ahead. Not only does daily inner renewal suggest it, and our present affliction is preparing it, but the very nature of faith itself guarantees it. "So we fix our eyes not on what is seen, but on what is unseen. For what is seen is temporary, but what is unseen is eternal" (2 Corinthians 4:18). Paul's argument here is very simple. The visible things of this life are but transient manifestations of abiding realities that cannot now be seen. If the transient form can exist, surely the reality behind it exists. The truly important thing is not the passing form but the eternal reality; consequently, the important thing in life is not to adjust oneself to the changing form, but to relate always to the abiding truth. It is the argument of Hebrews 11:8, 10, and 27—

> By faith Abraham . . . [looked] forward to the city with foundations, whose architect and builder is God. . . . By faith [Moses] left Egypt, not fearing the king's anger; he persevered because he saw him who is invisible.

The best is yet to be

Well, what is it, that is coming? Like a good chef, Paul has been whetting our appetites and stimulating our anticipation by veiled references to some breathtaking experience yet to come. But now he grows specific. In chapter five he describes the weight of glory in more explicit terms:

Now we know that if the earthly tent we live in is destroyed, we have a building from God, an eternal house in heaven, not built by human hands. Meanwhile we groan, longing to be clothed with our heavenly dwelling, because when we are clothed, we will not be found naked. For while we are in this tent, we groan and are burdened, because we do not wish to be unclothed but to be clothed with our heavenly dwelling, so that what is mortal may be swallowed up by life (2 Corinthians 5:1–4).

"A building from God"? "Not built by human hands"? "Our heavenly dwelling"? What do these expressions refer to? They are obviously set in direct contrast to the earthly tent we live in, our present body of flesh and bones. But before we take a closer look at these phrases, note how definite and certain Paul is. See how he begins: "We know . . . ." There is nothing uncertain about it at all.

Many today, as in the past, are trying to guess what lies beyond death. Some have supposed that the spirit of man departs, only to return in some reincarnation of life as another human being. The evidence used to support this is usually the testimony of certain persons (often given through a medium or in a hypnotic state) who apparently recall whole episodes from their previous existence. But it must be remembered that the Bible consistently warns of the existence of "lying spirits" or demons who have no compunctions about representing themselves to be the spirits of departed persons and who take delight in deceiving humans.

Others have suggested that knowledge of such things is put beyond us, that the only proper approach to life is to view everything as tentative, nothing can be depended on for sure. But Jesus and the apostles never speak that way. Christ said that He came to tell us the truth, that we might know. So Paul says here, *we know* certain things about life beyond death.

Well, what do we know? First, says Paul, we know that we now live in an earthly tent. Twice he calls the present body a tent. Tents are usually temporary dwellings. I once visited a family who lived in a tent in their yard while waiting for their new house to be finished. It wasn't very comfortable, but they were willing to put up with it until they could move into their real house. This is the case, Paul says, with Christians. They are living temporarily in tents.

Further, he says that in this tent we both groan and sigh. Do you ever listen to yourself when you get up in the morning? Do you ever groan? It is quite evident that the apostle is right, isn't it? Perhaps the tent is beginning to sag. The cords are loosening and the pegs are growing wobbly. There may also be the sigh of expectancy. "We groan and are burdened," says the apostle, "because we do not wish to be unclothed but to be clothed with our heavenly dwelling." No one wishes to be disembodied (which is what "unclothed" truly means), but nevertheless, we do long sometimes for something more than this body offers. We feel its limitations. Have you ever said when invited to do something, "I wish I could; the spirit is willing but the flesh is weak"? That is the sigh of anxiety, longing to be further clothed.

The heavenly house

In contrast to this temporary tent in which we now live, the apostle describes the permanent dwelling waiting for us when we die. It is "a building from God, an eternal house in heaven, not built by human hands."

This is the indescribable "ever-increasing glory" now being prepared for us by the trials and hardships we experience. If the present tent is our earthly body, then surely this permanent dwelling is the resurrection body, described in 1 Corinthians:

> So will it be with the resurrection of the dead. The body that is sown is perishable, it is raised imperishable; it is sown in dishonor, it is raised in glory; it is sown in weakness, it is raised in power; it is sown a natural body, it is raised a spiritual body. If there is a natural body, there is also a spiritual body (1 Corinthians 15:42–44).

If the apostle can describe our physical body as a tent, then it is surely fitting to describe the resurrection body as a house. A tent is temporary; a house is permanent. When we die, we will move from the temporary to the permanent; from the tent to the house, eternal in the heavens. This resurrection body is further described:

> The perishable must clothe itself with the imperishable, and the mortal with immortality. When the perishable has been clothed with the imperishable, and the mortal with immortality, then the saying that is written will come true: "Death has been swallowed up in victory." "Where, O death, is your victory? Where, O death, is your sting?" (1 Corinthians 15:53–55).

When we compare this passage with the one we are considering in 2 Corinthians 5, we note that the word for "clothed" (longing "to be *clothed* with our heavenly dwelling") is exactly the same Greek word as the one translated put on in 1 Corinthians 15 ("the perishable has been *clothed* with the imperishable"). This present perishable body of ours must be clothed with imperishable life, and this present mortal nature must be clothed with immortality. It is at that time, says Paul, that death is "swallowed up in victory." Compare that with the statement of 2 Corinthians 5, "that what is mortal may be swallowed up by life." The two passages are clearly parallel and the house "not built by human hands" is the resurrection body of 1 Corinthians 15.

But this poses a serious problem with some. They say, "Well, if the building of God is the resurrection body, then what does a believer live in while he is waiting for the resurrection body? Resurrection won't occur till the second coming of Jesus. What about the saints who have died through the centuries? Their bodies have been placed in the grave and won't arise until the resurrection; what do they live in during the interim?"

To this problem three widely varying answers have been posed. One is that departed saints have no bodies until the resurrection. They are with the Lord but as disembodied spirits, incomplete until regaining their bodies at the resurrection. But this view ignores Paul's words, "Meanwhile we groan, longing to be clothed with our heavenly dwelling, because when we are clothed, *we will not be found naked.* . . . We do not wish to be unclothed but to be clothed with our heavenly dwelling." Furthermore, the language of both 1 Corinthians 15 and 2 Corinthians 5 seems to imply an immediate donning of the resurrection body. There is no hint of any waiting period.

A second answer to the problem is that of soul sleep. This theory says that when a believer dies his soul remains asleep within the dead body. When the body is raised at the resurrection, the soul awakens. But because it has been asleep since death, it has no knowledge of the intervening time and no awareness of having been asleep. This concept solves the problem of the missing bodies but directly contravenes such Scriptures as the Lord's words to the thief on the cross, ""I tell you the truth, today you will be with me in paradise" (Luke 23:43), and Paul's declaration, "We are confident, I say, and would prefer to be away from the body and at home with the Lord" (2 Corinthians 5:8).

Still a third group proposes to solve the problem by suggesting that the house not made with human hands is not the resurrection body at all but an intermediate body God gives the believer to live in until the resurrection. Presumably, at that time, the intermediate body is dissolved and only the resurrection body exists. But it is difficult to square that with the description of the house not made with hands as being "an eternal house in heaven." Such a view also destroys the parallelism of 2 Corinthians 5 and 1 Corinthians 15. Since there is no hint anywhere in Scripture of the existence of an intermediate body, this view seems hardly tenable.

The problem disappears

The problem these strange answers propose to solve is really no problem at all. It arises only when we insist on projecting the concepts of time into eternity. We constantly think of heaven as a continuation on a larger and perfect scale of life on earth. Locked into our world of space and time, we find it very difficult to imagine life proceeding on any other terms. But we must remember that time is time and eternity is eternity and never the twain shall meet. We experience something of the same difficulty in dealing with the mathematical concept of infinity. Many people imagine infinity to be a very large number, but it is not. The difference is that if you subtract 1 from a very large number, you have one less, but if you subtract 1 from infinity you still have infinity.

Dr. Arthur Custance, a Canadian scientist who is also a remarkable Bible scholar and author of a series of biblical-scientific studies called *Doorway Papers*, has written something very helpful on this:

> The really important thing to notice is that Time stands in the same relation to Eternity, in one sense, as a large number does to infinity. There is one sense in which infinity includes a very large number, yet it is quite fundamentally different and independent of it. And by analogy, Eternity includes Time and yet is fundamentally something other. The reduction of Time until it gets smaller and smaller is still not Eternity. Nor do we reach Eternity by an extension of Time to great length. There is no direct pathway between Time and Eternity. They are different categories of experience.

(*Doorway Paper* No. 37. Published by the author.)

The thing we must remember in dealing with this matter of life beyond death is that when time ends, eternity begins. They are not the same, and we must not make them the same. Time means that we are locked into a pattern of chronological sequence which we are helpless to break. For example, all human beings sharing the same room will experience an earthquake together. While there are varying feelings and reactions, everyone will feel the earthquake at the same time. But in eternity events do not follow a sequential pattern. There is no past or future, only the present NOW. Within that NOW all events happen. An individual will experience sequence, but only in relationship to himself, and events will occur to him on the basis of his spiritual readiness. No two individuals need, therefore, experience the same event just because they happen to be together.

All this may sound quite confusing, and it is true it contains great elements of speculation. But let us return to the Scriptures and the problem of what happens to the believer at death. Because we hold firmly to the essential point that time and eternity are quite different, we believe then that the Christian who steps out of time steps into eternity. What was perhaps a far-off distant event in time is suddenly present in eternity if one is spiritually prepared for it. Since the one great event for which the Spirit of God is now preparing believers here on earth is the coming of Jesus Christ for His own, this is the event that greets every believer after death. It may be decades or even centuries before it breaks into time, but this particular person is no longer in time. He is in eternity. He sees "the Lord is coming with thousands upon thousands of his holy ones," just as Enoch did when he was permitted a look into eternity, and at a time when he was the seventh from Adam and the population of the earth was very small (Jude 14).

Where the ages meet

But what is even more amazing is that in the experience of that believer he does not leave anyone behind. All his loved ones who know Christ are there too, including his Christian descendants who were unborn when he died! Since there is no past or future in heaven, this must be the case. Even those who, in time, stand beside his grave and weep and then go home to an empty house, are, in his experience, with him in glory. Dr. Custance carries this even further.

> The experience of each saint is shared by all other saints, by those who have preceded and those who are to follow. For them all, all history, all intervening time between death and the Lord's return is suddenly annihilated so that each one finds to his amazement that Adam, too, is just dying and joining him on his way to meet the Lord: and Abraham and David, Isaiah and the Beloved John, Paul and Augustine, Hudson Taylor and you and I—all in one wonderful experience meeting the Lord in a single instant together, without precedence and without the slightest consciousness of delay, none being late and none too early.

(*Doorway Paper* No. 37, p. 28.)

This truly astonishing quality of eternity is the reason Jesus could promise his disciples with absolute certainty, "If I go and prepare a place for you, I will come back and take you to be with me that you also may be where I am" (John 14:3). Jesus' promise applied not only to that generation of Christians, but would apply to all, directly and personally, through all the intervening centuries. This also explains the strange promise at the close of Hebrews 11. Speaking of Abraham, Moses, David, Jacob, Joseph, and others, the writer says, "These were all commended for their faith, yet none of them received what had been promised. God had planned something better for us so that *only together with us would they be made perfect*" (Hebrews 11:39–40, emphasis added).

To be "made perfect" is to be resurrected, so this passage specifically states that the saints of old will not be resurrected without us. Either they are disembodied spirits waiting for the resurrection (which we have already seen is not likely) or there is some way by which we can leave time one by one and yet participate together in one glorious experience of resurrection. The proper understanding of eternity supplies the answer.

Eternity invades time

There are other references in Scripture that present this same phenomenon of the apparent eclipse of time. For instance, in Revelation 13:8, Jesus is referred to as "the Lamb that was slain from the creation of the world." Now the cross occurred at a precise moment of history. We know when the Lamb of God was slain. But the Bible says it occurred before the foundation of the world. How can an historical event, which occurred at a certain spot on earth, in the biblical reckoning be said to have occurred before the earth was even made? The passage does not say that the Lamb was foreordained to be slain before the foundation of the world, but it says He was actually slain then. Surely it means that the cross was an eternal event, taking place both in time and eternity. In time, it is long past; in eternity, it forever occurs.

The same is true of the resurrection and even the second coming of Christ. Any Christian who dies passes from the realm of time and space into time-lessness, into the NOW of God. This is when he experiences the full effect of these timeless events, to whatever degree his spiritual state requires. But the Lord's return is an event yet to take place in historical time when the church is complete and the end of the age has come. Perhaps this is the meaning of the Lord's words: "I tell you the truth, a time is coming and has now come when the dead will hear the voice of the Son of God and those who hear will live" (John 5:25).

A problem passage for some, in this respect, has been Revelation 6:9–11 where John sees the souls of those who had been slain for the Word of God under the altar in heaven. They are crying out to God, "How long, Sovereign Lord, holy and true, until you judge the inhabitants of the earth and avenge our blood?" In response they are told to be patient a little longer until the full count of martyrs is complete. This seems to indicate a sense of time in heaven and a need to wait for something in the future. How do we explain this in the light of what we have just seen regarding time and eternity?

The explanation, of course, is that John, who sees all this, is still a man living in time and space on earth. It is necessary, therefore, that what he sees in heaven be communicated to him in the symbols and language of earth. This is a common phenomenon in the book of Revelation. In the first chapter John sees Jesus in heaven. Does He really have long white hair and feet like burnished bronze and does a sharp sword come out of His mouth? No, clearly these are symbols which convey to John the power, wisdom, and glory of the Lord Jesus in His glorified, risen estate. The truth conveyed by the vision of the souls under the altar is evidently their identification with and concern for their brethren who are still on earth. They express themselves in terms of time and space in order that John (and we) may understand.

Creation on tiptoe

Perhaps this also indicates a further condition of the eternal experience: those who have stepped out of time into eternity can, if they so choose, step back into time again, though remaining invisible. That is, of course, exactly what Jesus did repeatedly during His forty-day post-resurrection ministry. To those in eternity, time may be like a book on a library bookshelf. If we choose, we can pick up and browse through it at random. We can enter the time sequence found in the book at any place we desire, follow it through for as long as we like, and then lay it down to reenter (in consciousness) the time sequence in which we normally live. In similar fashion those in eternity may select some period of history that they would like to live through and step back into that time, living out its events, though invisibly. This, of course, is pure speculation and may not prove to be true at all, but it does at least fit the suggestion of Scripture that in a resurrected state we will be free from many of the limitations of our present body of flesh.

One thing is clear. Paul looked forward with eager anticipation to the day when he would put off his earthly tent and move into his heavenly dwelling. It would be, he says, a spiritual body, not meaning, as many have supposed, a body made up of spirit— something rather ghostly and immaterial—but rather a body fully subject to the spirit, designed expressly for the spirit. In this life, we are forced to say, "The spirit is willing, but the flesh is weak." But in the life to come, we can say, "My spirit is willing and the flesh is equal to its demands. Let's go!" Perhaps a quote from C. S. Lewis will help us understand this point:

> The command *Be ye perfect* is not idealistic gas. Nor is it a command to do the impossible. He is going to make us into creatures that can obey that command. He said (in the Bible) that we

were "gods" and He is going to make good His words. If we let Him—for we can prevent Him, if we choose—He will make the feeblest and filthiest of us into a god or goddess, a dazzling, radiant, immortal creature, pulsating all through with such energy and joy and wisdom and love as we cannot now imagine, a bright stainless mirror which reflects back to God perfectly (though, of course, on a smaller scale) His own boundless power and delight and goodness. The process will be long and in parts very painful; but that is what we are in for. Nothing less. He meant what He said.

(*Mere Christianity,* p. 171)

Yes, something more is coming—something so different from anything we have known up to now that it defies description. Yet it is something so splendid and glorious that, even whispered, it sends chills of expectation down the spine of the universe. Phillips' version of Romans 8:18–19 is beautifully expressive of this: "In my opinion whatever we may have to go through now is less than nothing compared with the magnificent future God has in store for us. The whole creation is on tiptoe to see the wonderful sight of the sons of God coming into their own."

The courageous life
Lest we become so enraptured with this splendid future that we lose all interest in the present, the apostle wisely reminds us that the key to this future is in our present experience.

Now it is God who has made us for this very purpose and has given us the Spirit as a deposit, guaranteeing what is to come. Therefore we are always confident and know that as long as we are at home in the body we are away from the Lord. We live by faith, not by sight. We are confident, I say, and would prefer to be away from the body and at home with the Lord (2 Corinthians 5:5–8).

Twice in this passage Paul says that a clear view of the coming glory should mean that our present life is marked with good courage. Surely that means more than keeping a stiff upper lip. Rather, it means to be full of encouragement, to be joyful, expectant, confident. He gives two reasons for this. First, in preparing us for the glory to come God has given us the Holy Spirit as His guarantee. We do not need to doubt that the resurrection of our body is ahead, for the presence within us of the Spirit of resurrection makes it sure.

Remember that in 2 Corinthians 4 the apostle says, "we know that the one who raised the Lord Jesus from the dead will also raise us with Jesus" (vs. 14). The Spirit knows how to resurrect dead bodies, for He has already done it once. Also, the Spirit has not only effected the resurrection of the body of Jesus but He has also been resurrecting our spirits every day since we became Christians. "Though outwardly we are wasting away, yet inwardly we are being renewed day by day." How many times has the Spirit brought you back from a sense of death and darkness to renewed life, interest, and vitality? That power to renew is our guarantee that God will bring us to glory.

The operative principle

The second reason for confidence in the present hour is that though the resurrection life will be amazing beyond description, it is nevertheless true that we are learning how to handle the resurrection body by the way we handle our present body now. Though resurrection will be something new, it will not be *entirely* new; even though it will be strange, it won't be that strange. C. S. Lewis has said that these present bodies are given to us much as ponies are given to English schoolboys—to learn to ride "the ponies" in order to be ready for the glorious stallions that are even now arching their necks and pawing the floor in the heavenly stables.

What is it we are learning now that will be so necessary then? It is to walk by faith and not by sight! That is the operative principle of eternity, and we must learn it here. Certain hymns have reflected the idea that when we get to heaven we will no longer need to walk by faith but can then walk by sight. It is true that we will then "see" the Lord, but that in no way will eliminate our need to respond to Him. In fact, it will increase it! Faith is the human response to a divine offer. As we live by means of Christ now—by faith in Him—so we will need to live by means of Christ then, by responding to his life and love.

It is for this reason that Paul uses the term "at home" to describe both our present experience in an earthly body and the coming experience when we are "with the Lord." We are now "at home" in the body, though away from the Lord. Then we shall be away from the body, but "at home" with the Lord. In either case, we are "at home."

All our tenderest associations gather around the word *home*. It is where we feel relaxed, at ease, natural. And when we step into the stunning glory awaiting us, we will feel the same way—at home, relaxed, at ease, because we have not changed our basic nature. At home, here in the body, we are learning to walk by faith in a way that feels natural and comfortable. At home with the Lord, it will be the same.

This was Paul's own experience in that strange episode he recounts for us in 2 Corinthians 12. There he says he was caught up in the third heaven, the very Paradise of God. But twice he says he did not know whether he was in the body or out of it. Though the experience was beyond description and he heard and saw things he could not utter, it was not unnatural. Paul was simply not aware of his body.

He was too much at home to notice.

Our Highest Motivation

A NOBLEMAN'S SON once complained that he didn't know what to do with his life. "Father," he said, "what should my ambition be? What should I make of myself? What should I do in life?"

"When I was your age," said the nobleman, "I wondered about the very same questions. But over the years, I've learned something that may be of help to you. I suggest that if you want to have an interesting life, just become a friend of the king—then wait and see what happens."

Those are wise words for us as Christians. Many Christians are looking for their calling, their grand ambition, their great motivation in life—when all they really need to have a great, adventure-filled life is to simply become a friend of the King, then wait and see what happens. God does not want His people standing on one foot, agonizing over how to discover His will. He has made His will very plain in Scripture. He just wants us to go out into the world and start doing it!

"So we make it our goal to please him," writes Paul in 2 Corinthians 5:9, "whether we are at home in the body or away from it." Pleasing God is the proper occupation of the Christian for both time and eternity. We are learning to do it here on earth; we shall perform it perfectly there, in eternity. To please God always requires faith, for "without faith it is impossible to please God" (Hebrews 11:6). As we have already seen, to walk by faith is to live on the basis of the new covenant, continually accepting the judgment of the cross as to the flesh and choosing to act in dependence upon the resurrecting life of the Spirit. "It is we who are the circumcision, we who worship by the Spirit of God, who glory in Christ Jesus, and who put no confidence in the flesh" (Philippians 3:3).

It is helpful to us to learn that the will of God which many Christians are seeking to fulfill is not so much concerned with *what* we do as it is with *how* we do it. God does direct us at times to certain activities or places, though often He will leave the choice up to us. But what He is continually concerned about is the resource we are counting upon for success in whatever we do. To depend upon "something coming from us" is to be displeasing to God, no matter what the activity may be. To do even a simple task (sweeping the floor, for instance), counting upon "everything coming from God" is to be infinitely pleasing to Him. This is why Jesus was pleased with the widow's mite and with the offer of the loaves and fishes. Each of these incidents was a presenting of a simple object to God with the expectation that He would do something with it. That is faith. That is what pleases God.

What will move me?

But the real problem of the Christian life is not how to discover the will of God. We have known that problem, to one degree or another, all our lives. The real problem is to want to do it! It is the problem of motivation. That problem remains, even after we have discovered what it really is that God wants. I can know a great deal about the Christian life: I can know that the true purpose for my life is to please God; I can even know just what it is that will please Him (faith); and I can remember in times past the pleasure it gave me to please God and the blessings that followed. Yet, confronted by the lure of the flesh, the pleasure of sin, and the ease with which it could all be justified (a veil), I can deliberately choose to disobey God. I have done it many times. And so, I'm sure, have you.

When the soul swings in the balance between truth and error, good and evil, what will tip the scale in the right direction? That is the real problem. It is the issue of motivation.

As with everything else in the Christian life, God has not left us without help at this point. Two powerful forces act upon us to stabilize our wavering wills and draw us back from the alluring brink. They are like motors to move us into right action. The word "motor" comes from the same root as motive. Now, to choose is our inherent human function, but to choose *rightly* demands that a force operate within us that will firmly turn us and propel us in the right direction. Paul describes these forces to us. The first, perhaps rather surprisingly, is fear.

> We must all appear before the judgment seat of Christ, that each one may receive what is due him for the things done while in the body, whether good or bad. Since, then, we know what it is to fear the Lord, we try to persuade men. What we are is plain to God, and I hope it is also plain to your conscience (2 Corinthians 5:10–11).

Our Highest Motivation   159

Somehow the idea has grown among Christians that fear is an improper motive; that if it is accepted at all, it is base and inferior. But Scripture never takes that position. Everywhere, from Genesis to Revelation, and especially in Genesis and Revelation, the fear of the Lord is extolled as a very proper and highly desirable motive for living. In fact, it is regarded as foundational. "The fear of the LORD is the beginning of knowledge, but fools despise wisdom and discipline" (Proverbs 1:7). The psalmist exhorts us, "Fear the LORD, you his saints, for those who fear him lack nothing" (Psalm 34:9), and declares that a man reaches a stage of great danger when there is "no fear of God before his eyes" (Psalm 36:1). It should not surprise us, therefore, that Paul speaks first of fear when he sets before us the great motives of life.

But what comes to mind when we think of fearing God? Is it some abject, cringing, expression of terror like a dog crawling in fear to his offended master? Such fear is inspired by guilt, and guilt has absolutely no place in a believer's relationship to God. Is it the fear born of hate that strikes back at God with defiance and anger when a divine demand is faced? No, hate, too, is no longer a viable motive in the life of a Christian. Then perhaps it is the fear that God will let us down—a lack of trust that makes the heart anxious and restless. No, these are unrealistic and unhealthy fears. The fear of which Paul speaks is something that is still there when a believer stands as a son before his loving Father, with a bold and confident spirit, making his requests known to him. It is a fear that finds its focus at the judgment seat of Christ.

This judgment tribunal is presented in Scripture as awaiting the believer who steps out of time into eternity. "Judge nothing before the appointed time; wait till the Lord comes. He will bring to light what is hidden in darkness and will expose the motives of men's hearts. At that time each will receive his praise from God" (1 Corinthians 4:5). It is a time when "each one may receive what is due him for the things done while in the body, whether good or bad" (2 Corinthians 5:10). These verses seem to suggest an occasion when our entire earthly life passes in review before us and we learn—perhaps for the first time!—what has been pleasing to God and what has not. It will undoubtedly be a time of great surprises. Many things we felt were acceptable to God and profitable to us will be found to be spoiled by improper or wrongful dependence. At the same time, God will single out many forgotten or seemingly insignificant acts as greatly pleasing to Him.

The secrets of the heart

In line with what we have seen in the last chapter, there is a sense in which this judgment is going on in our lives right now. "If we judged ourselves, we would not come under judgment. When we are judged by the Lord, we are being disciplined so that we will not be condemned with the world" (1 Corinthians 11:31–32). Eternal life has already possessed our spirits and is gradually reclaiming our souls. Consequently, the judgment seat of Christ, which is part of eternity, has already begun.

As we progress in the Christian life, we learn increasingly to understand that "What is highly valued among men is detestable in God's sight" (Luke 16:15). Increasingly we judge ourselves on this basis. We learn to obey the words of Jesus to pray and fast and give alms in secret, knowing that the God who sees in secret will grant a reward. But if we do things "to be seen by men," we already have all the reward we will get.

Paul also speaks of this in 1 Corinthians 3:11–15:

> No one can lay any foundation other than the
> one already laid, which is Jesus Christ. If any
> man builds on this foundation using gold, silver,
> costly stones, wood, hay or straw, his work will
> be shown for what it is, because the Day will
> bring it to light. It will be revealed with fire, and
> the fire will test the quality of each man's work.
> If what he has built survives, he will receive his
> reward. If it is burned up, he will suffer loss; he
> himself will be saved, but only as one escaping
> through the flames.

Wood, hay, and straw are highly combustible and all
grow from the earth—an apt figure for those works of
the flesh that arise out of our natural life and are
therefore rejected by God. Gold, silver, and costly
stones, however, are noncombustible and, though found
in the earth, are not a part of it—another apt figure, but
this time it is a figure of the deeds done of the Spirit,
which alone are able to survive this test of fire and are
acceptable in the eyes of God.

The "fear of the Lord" that Paul connects with this
sobering judgment comes from an awareness that God
cannot be fooled or deceived in any way. It springs from
the fact that God views us with stark and naked
realism, and that since He is no respecter of persons, we
cannot count on privilege or favor for some special
consideration before Him. He is not swayed by our
emotional pleas nor moved by our tears to change His
evaluation. Our explanations and justifications made so
easily before ourselves or other people will die un-
uttered on our lips in the presence of Christ's immu-
table majesty. His judgment will be inescapable and

without appeal. Before the white light of those loving eyes, all pretenses will fall away and we shall see ourselves as He has always seen us: "Then shall I know fully, even as also I am known" (1 Corinthians 13:12 KJV).

Don't waste it

It is this truth—the certainty that he will one day face the searching gaze of his Lord and Savior—that motivates Paul to serve Jesus and persuade men. He does not wish to waste his life. He knows that with his keen mind, his strong and dominant personality, and his powers of persuasion he could easily achieve a record of influence and accomplishments that would impress the world and other Christians. He might easily become very wealthy or gain great prestige and fame. He had the natural gifts to take him to the top of whatever heap he should decide to climb. But what would it all mean at the judgment seat of Christ? Nothing! A sheer waste of time and effort! It would only be what Paul describes to the Galatians as "making a good impression," nothing but wood, hay, and stubble, consumed in a flash by the eternal fire of God.

To him, life is a great race, an endurance contest, which he is running, not against others but against himself. The goal he sees drawing ever nearer is his death or departure to be with Christ; the prize is the resurrection glory which awaits him there. The object of the race is to take each step in dependence upon the Spirit of God and not upon the energy of the flesh. Paul's passsion is clear: "To me, to live is Christ," is his passion.

Once, after a Billy Graham crusade meeting, I slipped into a seat on a bus beside a young man who had gone forward in the meeting that night and given his heart to Christ. I spoke to him of what his new life would mean and, among other things, mentioned that he could now be free from all fear of death. He turned and looked me in the eye and said with all sincerity, "I have never been much afraid of death. But I'll tell you what I am afraid of—I'm afraid I'll waste my life."

I believe that fear is deep within each of us. It has been put there by our Creator. No one wants to waste his or her life. When we understand the terms by which the value of that life is measured, we find it to be a great force to help us choose the right and reject the wrong. "What we are is plain to God, and I hope it is also plain to your conscience" (2 Corinthians 5:11). Thus Paul seeks to persuade the Corinthians to walk as he walked with the bright light of the judgment seat of Christ on his path.

The supreme motive

But there is a motive even greater than the motive of fear. Another force at work in our lives has power to move us even when the fear of wasting our lives leaves us unmoved (as it sometimes will). Paul now goes on to declare that greatest of all motives:

> We are not trying to commend ourselves to you again, but are giving you an opportunity to take pride in us, so that you can answer those who take pride in what is seen rather than in what is in the heart. If we are out of our mind, it is for the sake of God; if we are in our right mind, it is for you. For Christ's love compels us, because we are convinced that one died for all, and therefore all died. And he died for all, that those who live should no longer live for themselves but for him who died for them and was raised again (2 Corinthians 5:12–15).

164   **Authentic Christianity**

Paul's behavior as a Christian was a source of bafflement to many at the church in Corinth. They could not understand his approach, and his motives were forever being questioned. He explains the reason for their perplexity in his first letter: "Brothers, I could not address you as spiritual but as worldly—mere infants in Christ" (1 Corinthians 3:1). His actions seemed strange to them because they didn't understand the new covenant. They expected him to act and react to situations just as they did—and they were confused and baffled when he did not conform. It is clear from the above passage and others in the Corinthian letters that they expected him to boast of his exploits on behalf of Christ and to find subtle ways to commend himself before them, for this is what they did. But now he insists he is not doing this, though it might at first appear to be the case.

Rather, he explains that the force prompting him to act contrary to the usual ways of the world is not arising from a secret ambition for position. No, it originates from Christ within: "Christ's love compels us," urges us, drives us (2 Corinthians 5:14). Because of what Paul says in this chapter, we know that some people actually claimed Paul was insane because of his intense devotion to the ministry of Jesus Christ and because of his unexpected behavior. Paul repeats some of the charges that have been leveled at him—but he declares the method in his madness, as the current saying goes. "If we are out of our mind, it is for the sake of God," he says in verse 13. "If we are in our right mind, it is for you."

Even though many people found it hard to explain Paul's actions, Paul could state clearly that his own objective was right. All of his behavior, whether crazy or sane, was focused on serving Christ and influencing people for Christ. Paul's goal could be anticipated when it was understood that the love of Christ urged him on. His actions were the actions of love, directed to the glory of God and the service of men, never for the advancement of self!

Now, *that* is always highly suspicious behavior! The person who has no axe to grind, no angle for his own profit, is behaving very strangely. The world expects people to "look out for Number One." The world also knows that everyone who is smart hides his self-interest until the last possible moment. He always *appears* to be concerned for the welfare of others, even while he is trying to manipulate the situation to his own advantage. That is why one frequently hears, "Okay, what's your angle?" or "All right, what's the catch?" Most Christians also reflect this view, despite their high-sounding "Christianese."

Finding someone who consistently, in varying circumstances, behaves contrary to this basic human principle may cause some to be perplexed and unbelieving. What is the answer? "Love is the explanation," Paul says in effect. "The love of Christ presses us, urges us on, takes hold of us and overpowers our natural self-interest, and makes us act contrary to nature." A death and a resurrection have occurred, he argues. "We are convinced that one died for all, and therefore all died." When Christ became what we are, He died, and, therefore, we who are in Christ have died with Him. The natural life has been shown to be worthless, totally unprofitable.

But there is more. "And he died for all, that those who live should *no longer live for themselves* but for him who died for them and was raised again" (2 Corinthians 5:15, emphasis added). If we died with Him, we also rose with Him, and the risen life we now live is different from the old life. It is no longer self-centered, loving itself supremely. It is outward-directed. It reaches out to others naturally and without self-consciousness. It is not a put-on but real. Whenever we yield to the love of Christ, says Paul, that is the way we act, and His love is the reason we act that way. Once we have yielded to that love we cannot help being self-giving, for that is the way His love is. The love of Christ controls us.

An article that appeared in *Christianity Today* a number of years ago described the Christlike love of Christians who were undergoing persecution and imprisonment for their faith. A former criminal, Kozlov, converted to Christ and became a leader in the persecuted church. In the article, he wrote this about life in a Soviet prison:

> Among the general despair, while prisoners like myself were cursing ourselves, the camp, the authorities; while we opened up our veins, or our stomachs, or hanged ourselves; the Christians (often with sentences of twenty to twenty-five years) did not despair. One could see Christ reflected in their faces. Their pure, upright life, deep faith and devotion to God, their gentleness and their wonderful manliness, became a shining example of real life for thousands (*Christianity Today,* June 21, 1974).

That is authentic Christianity. You find it under the worst, most horrifying circumstances imaginable. We should certainly be able to find it in our homes and our churches today.

A trinity of love

Some people wonder, "What does Paul mean when he says, 'Christ's love compels us'? Is it Christ's love for

Paul, Paul's love for Christ, or Christ's love flowing out of Paul to others?" The question is a valid one, and we are not given much help from the Greek text. It will allow any of the above meanings. But a verse in John's letter serves as a guide to interpreting Paul's meaning. It suggests where love begins. "This is love: not that we loved God, but that he loved us and sent his Son as an atoning sacrifice for our sins" (1 John 4:10).

Love begins with God, not with us. Christ loved us first; even, says Paul in Romans 5, while we were yet sinners and enemies of God. His love for us, accepted by faith, awakens our love for him so that Peter can write, "Though you have not seen him, you love him" (1 Peter 1:8). Paul agrees with this, "God has poured out his love into our hearts by the Holy Spirit, whom he has given us" (Romans 5:5).

When our hearts have been stirred and awakened by God's love, we are ready to reach out in love to our fellowmen, disregarding our own interests. "We loved you so much that we were delighted to share with you not only the gospel of God but our lives as well, because you had become so dear to us" (1 Thessalonians 2:8).

It takes all three phases to fully manifest the love of Christ. But the important point to see is that love, not duty, is the proper motive for Christian functioning. "If you love me, you will obey what I command" (John 14:15), says Jesus. It is not the other way around: "If you keep my commandments you will love me." This is also seen in Paul's frequent exhortations to very practical duties, "Husbands, love your wives," "Wives, submit to your husbands," "Masters, treat your servants justly and fairly," but never without a reference to the motive that should urge them: "For the Lord Jesus Christ's sake," "As to the Lord."

Love makes obedience easy; it is the delight of love to do what the loved one desires. Therefore, when the heart grows dull and obedience is difficult, the proper response of the Christian is not to grit his teeth and decide to tough it out but to remember who it is that asks this of him, and then for His sake to do it. When a Christian responds this way, he will find to his amazement that his own attitude has changed. A new outlook is born within him. That is what Paul describes in 2 Corinthians 5:16–17:

> So from now on we regard no one from a worldly point of view. Though we once regarded Christ in this way, we do so no longer. Therefore, if anyone is in Christ, he is a new creation; the old has gone, the new has come!

Perhaps the clearest evidence that the new covenant is in operation is the change it makes in our view of others. No longer does position, caste, color, sex, or wealth matter. Everyone is seen to be of infinite worth because he is made in the image of God and can be redeemed through Christ. Nothing else really matters. Paul seems to suggest here that there was a time when he knew Christ "after the flesh." Does that mean that he heard Jesus teach and preach and perhaps had even met Him? It seems likely. If that is the case, a drastic change had occurred in his outlook.

The new view

A British Bible teacher and evangelist, Major Ian Thomas, has described that change so brilliantly that I want to reproduce it.

> Paul, the apostle says, "There was a time when, as Saul of Tarsus, I made my own reasonable

estimate of this man called Jesus Christ, about whom I had heard so much. When I did so I wasn't unkind; I wasn't even prejudiced. I applied all the normal, reasonable methods of evaluation of my own day and I came to my own conclusions about Jesus Christ. This was what I found:

"FAMILY BACKGROUND? A nobody! I had to agree with my theological colleagues that he was the illegitimate son of a faithless woman who was not only faithless but a liar.

"FAMILY BREEDING? In common with all my comrades, I couldn't help coming to the conclusion that he was worth precisely nothing. He had absolutely no standing in his community.

"PROFESSIONAL STANDING? I went into that pretty thoroughly. I discovered that he had no formal education; he was brought up in a peasant's home; he was an apprentice at a carpenter's bench; eventually he got through his apprenticeship and became a carpenter. In terms of professional status, I came to the reasonable, logical conclusion that he was worth absolutely *nothing!*

"THEOLOGICAL BACKGROUND? He professed to be a preacher, but I discovered that, by all reasonable human estimates, here again he amounted to nothing. He hadn't been to college; he hadn't been to seminary; he hadn't had any instruction whatever from the ecclesiastical dignitaries of our day; he had sat at nobody's feet. Professionally he was *nothing.* He was but a tub-thumping rabble-rouser and an incorrigible street preacher. In terms of the ecclesiastical situation of my day and generation he was simply a nobody.

"MONEY? He was born in a borrowed stable; when he wanted to give an illustration he even had to borrow a coin; he rode around on a borrowed donkey; when he wanted to celebrate the Passover he sent on a messenger and managed to persuade somebody to make his home available; he always lived in other people's homes. He was, on all the reasonable human basis upon which we can justifiably come to a conclusion, an incorrigible scrounger. He even died on a borrowed cross and was buried in a borrowed tomb. In terms of property or wealth he was worth absolutely *nothing*.

"But something happened to me, Saul of Tarsus, on the road to Damascus. Breathing out threatenings and slaughter, I was going to throw into jail and have put to death anyone who dared to perpetuate the myth that this *incorrigible nothing* was the Christ of God.

"Then, suddenly, there was a light brighter than the sun at noonday. I was blinded. I fell to my face. I was helpless. And I heard a voice, saying, 'Saul, Saul, why do you persecute me?' 'Who are you, Lord?' I said. 'I am Jesus, whom you are persecuting.'

"Then I learned that the one I had thought to be nothing, was NOTHING BUT GOD, MANIFEST IN THE FLESH. By my human evaluation *he was nothing* and as Saul of Tarsus *I was everything*. But on the road to Damascus I discovered that *he became everything and I became nothing*.

"Now I have such knowledge of him that I no longer know him from a human point of view which once I considered to be valid. Now, *to me, to live is Christ*."

[*Used by permission.*]

Yes, life as a Christian is totally, radically, different. Impelled by the twin motives of the fear of God and the love of Christ, it goes counter to the normal impulses of life. It is that new creation, envisioned by the prophets, *already begun!* Right in the midst of the decay of the old creation, the new is rising. Eternity is invading time. Urged on, driven, and mastered by love, we will continue to swim against the current of this darkening age until the day breaks and the shadows flee.

The Glory of Ministry

SHARING THE GOOD NEWS of Jesus Christ with others is a very simple matter. It has been beautifully and simply described as, "One beggar telling another where to find bread." That is so true! I am a beggar. You are a beggar. Every human being alive on this planet is a beggar! Whether we are Christians or non-Christians makes no difference: Our own righteousness is like the filthy rags of a starving beggar (see Isaiah 64:6), and we are all equally lost in our poverty and sin—apart from God. A Christian beggar differs from a non-Christian beggar in only one respect: He has found the Bread of Life, Jesus Christ. When we, as Christians, witness about Jesus, we do not do so from any position of superiority or self-righteousness. We are simply poor beggars telling other beggars where they can find the same Bread we have found!

Sharing Christ does not require a formal or stylized presentation, nor does it require a special place or time. It is not restricted to those who are ordained or are "in the ministry." Every person who has experienced true Christianity is already in the ministry because he or she possesses what others desperately need.

The authentic Christian life is essentially and radically different from the natural life lived by a man or woman of the world. Outwardly, it can be very much the same: involved with making a living, going to school, getting married, raising children, mowing lawns, buying groceries, getting along with neighbors. But inwardly, the basis of living is dramatically different. Christ is a part of all these things! He is the motivator of every wholesome action, the corrector of every wrong deed or thought. He is the giver of every joy and the healer of every hurt. He is no longer merely on the *edges* of life, acknowledged on Sunday but absent through the week. Christ is the *center* of everything. Life revolves around Him. As a consequence, life comes into proper focus, a deep peace possesses the heart, strength grips the spirit despite outward trials, and kindness and joy radiate abroad. This is really living!

Once we truly understand and appreciate what Jesus Christ has done for us, it is impossible to keep it a secret! The wonderful story of new life in Christ absolutely shouts within us, demanding to be shared with others who still struggle with guilt, despair, shame, and hostility. Whenever we see another hurting human being, we know we have an opportunity for sharing. This is our ministry—an abundant ministry, available to all, as simple and as natural as breathing. The apostle Paul describes this ministry in these words:

> All this is from God, who reconciled us to himself through Christ and gave us the ministry of reconciliation: that God was reconciling the world to himself in Christ, not counting men's sins

against them. And he has committed to us the message of reconciliation (2 Corinthians 5:18–19).

Four times in this brief statement Paul stresses the word "reconciliation." Since man was designed to be indwelt by God, nothing could be more damaging to our humanity than to be estranged from the God who made us. Alienation from God is the fundamental sickness of humanity, and it breaks out in such hurtful expressions as guilt, hostility, despair, and even addiction (twelve-step treatment programs for alcoholism and drug addiction are based on the fact that people use these substances to fill the God-shaped void in their lives).

The best news humanity could ever hear is that some means of reconciliation with God has been found. It is the great privilege of Christians to declare this good news to those who desperately need it and who are willing to listen because of the hurts and holes in their own lives. Effective witness almost always begins at the point of need. "Come to me, all you who are weary and burdened," says Jesus, "and I will give you rest" (Matthew 11:28).

Certain elements of this ministry are underscored by Paul to indicate its greatness and its relevance. To review these is to become aware of the immense privilege of proclaiming such a message to hurting— and even hurtful!—men and women.

The ministry of reconciliation originates with God. "All this is from God," says Paul. The offended one, God Himself, initiates the way of reconciliation. We, the offenders, only respond.

The good news does not originate with man; it is not simply another way man has invented to find his own way back to God. The very nature of the good news is such that it couldn't have been invented by man. It begins by postulating nothing in man except weakness, failure, and rebellion. By that one stroke, all competition is eliminated in the quest for salvation. No one can properly think of himself as any closer to God than other people—apart from Christ. Those who pride themselves on their moral and respectable lives are no closer to God than the murderer or the sex pervert, for in reality, pride of respectability is just as much a manifestation of alienation from God as murder or debauchery.

This element of the good news irritates and offends many people. Those who count on their good works to save them are put off by this proclamation. They want God to take them on their terms. However, their offense is only further confirmation of the apostle's claim that "all this is from God." No flagrant sinner would dare dream he has some way to stand before God; no self-righteous person would imagine he needed anything to make himself acceptable. The good news of reconciliation could never originate with man. It comes wholly from God.

The ministry of reconciliation is personally experienced. The Christian who witnesses to the new covenant does not speak academically. He is able to identify fully with the hurt and darkness of those to whom he speaks, for he has (as the saying goes) "been there, done that" himself. But he has found something else, something so satisfying and complete as to make him eager to share it with others. He doesn't speak of "the plan of salvation" as though it were all theological doctrine, requiring only an intellectual grasp in order to receive it. Rather, he gives witness of a personal Lord who is at once the

Savior and sustainer of his life. He does not convey the impression that when he surrendered to this Lord he was immediately and completely delivered from all struggle with evil, guilt, hate, and fear, but he makes it clear that the initial surrender produced a permanent change of heart. And power continually flows from that center to enable him to conquer—gradually, successively, day by day, step by step—the areas of his life yet dominated by evil and failure. He freely acknowledges his present failures but rejoices in the certainty that they too shall succumb to the authority and power of a resurrected Lord. "Sin shall not be your master, because you are not under law, but under grace" (Romans 6:14).

The ministry of reconciliation is universally inclusive. "[God] gave us the ministry of reconciliation. . . . God was reconciling the world to himself in Christ." One of the wonders of true Christianity is its universality. Though the church was originally Jewish, it was quickly embraced by the Gentiles. Christianity spread from the Holy Land into Europe and Africa, to Asia and the Americas. It has proven to satisfy the spiritual hunger of people from every culture and ethnic background, from every class—rich, poor, and in-between. Jesus is worshiped in the penthouses and in the ghettos, by those of the political right, left, and center. Men find that the message of Jesus speaks to their need as men, and women find that the message of Jesus fulfills and completes their femininity. It brings the wholeness of God to the whole need of every person—physically, spiritually, and emotionally.

The silly idea has arisen somehow that Jesus and God the Father have different and opposing personalities. According to this idea, Jesus is tender and compassionate toward lost mankind, and stands protectively between us and a vengeful, angry God the Father. Paul disposes of this faulty concept forever with his clear statement, "God was reconciling the world to himself in Christ." It was the Father who initiated the work of redemption. He gave His only Son, sending Him into the world to bring about our redemption and reconciliation through cruel death and subsequent resurrection. It was the Father who "did not spare his own Son, but gave him up for us all" (Romans 8:32).

So it is the Father *and* the Son who, by means of the Spirit, reach out to a hurting, lonely world and offer pardon, peace, and joy to all who will come. No one is excluded by virtue of race, color, condition, or class. The door is wide open to all.

The ministry of reconciliation is without condemnation. "Not counting men's sins against them." Because of the cross of Jesus, the problem human evil raises before God is totally eliminated. God does not require anything but the honest acknowledgment of evil to eliminate its degrading, destructive results in people's lives. No penance is demanded, nor will any be accepted. No self-chastisement is required. Any attempt to resort to these is but proof that the individual has not believed what God has plainly said. This is true not only when a person first comes to Christ, but it remains true throughout his entire life.

The penalty of death for any or all of my sins has already been fully borne by Christ—and that means death in all its varied forms. I bear my own sins when I refuse to believe God and seek in some way to justify them before God. But the experience of death ends the moment I believe Him: "Therefore, there is now no condemnation for those who are in Christ Jesus" (Romans 8:1).

This is the element that especially makes reconciliation such good news. All God ever requires of us is that we acknowledge our evil and be willing to be delivered from its power. God accomplishes the actual *work* of deliverance for us on the basis of Jesus' death. The cross has *already* set us free; it is only waiting for us to believe it to become real in our experience.

Of course, certain natural consequences of our evil will still remain. Sin always leaves its scars. The person who repents from a lifestyle of sexual sin and turns to Christ will be forgiven—but forgiveness doesn't erase the natural consequences of that lifestyle, such as broken relationships, emotional scars, or sexually transmitted diseases. The person who repents from a life of criminal behavior and turns to Christ will be forgiven—but forgiveness doesn't erase the possibility of punishment for those crimes and the need to make restitution. The consequences of old sins, even though forgiven, often remain. But those sins can no longer produce spiritual death in us, because the resurrection life of Jesus now pulsates within us. The mistakes and rebellions of our past will be turned into instruments of grace to mellow and soften us and make us clearer and brighter manifestations of God's redeeming love.

We should never hesitate to return to God when we sin. He is already fully aware of our sin. In fact, He expects us to fail, because He knows us better than we know ourselves. Like the loving father of the prodigal son, He is not ashamed of us, nor does He reject us. He waits for our return, and when we do, He welcomes us with a father's kiss and with open arms.

An innocent man was once on trial for his life in a court of law. After the evidence was presented by both the prosecution and the defense, the prosecuting attorney rose to give his summation to the jury. He spoke at great length and with persuasive eloquence, citing all the evidence against the accused man. When the prosecutor had concluded his speech, the innocent man leaned over to his own attorney and whispered, "He was very convincing. For a while there, he even had *me* believing I was guilty!"

Satan is much like that prosecutor. He accuses us, making us feel guilty even after our sins have been completely washed away by the sacrifice of Jesus, even after God has pronounced us innocent because of the cross. As Christians, forgiven by God, we may at times experience shame, we may feel unworthy—but those emotions come from our accuser, Satan. They do not come from God. Our loving heavenly Father has already forgiven us and waits only for us to acknowledge our sin and thank Him for the restored relationship that is already ours through Jesus Christ.

The ministry of reconciliation is personally delivered. "He has committed to us the message of reconciliation." The good news does not come by means of angels. It is not announced from heaven by loud, impersonal voices. It doesn't even come by poring over dusty volumes from the past. In each generation it is delivered by living, breathing men and women who speak from their own experience. Incarnation, the word become flesh, is forever God's way of truly communicating with people. It comes always at the cost of hunger and thirst, personal hardship borne for Christ's sake—blood, sweat, and tears.

Some today have claimed to come to Christ apart from the aid of others, having read the good news in the Scriptures without the aid of teachers. But they have forgotten the labors and hardships endured by those who have given them the Scriptures in their own language, often at the cost of their lives. No one who reads the Bible in English should ever forget that Tyndale, Wycliffe, and Coverdale, the early translators, were all bitterly persecuted men who labored at the risk of their own lives.

It is easily demonstrable today that only a few Christians are able to read the Scriptures and grow by direct obedience to the precepts stated there. The rest of us seem to require models and mentors to follow. Only a few have the gift of faith, daring to challenge the accepted norms and traditions in the church that violate God's Word. But when those few lead out and exemplify in their lives the blessing that comes from obedience to the Scriptures, others are able to follow. Love and faith must somehow become visible, embodied in human lives, before they can be caught and emulated by others. "We loved you so much that we were delighted to share with you not only the gospel of God but our lives as well, because you had become so dear to us" (1 Thessalonians 2:8). The gospel contains a strong personal element that cannot be eliminated without diminishing and harming its effect.

The ministry of reconciliation is authoritatively accredited. "We are therefore Christ's ambassadors, as though God were making his appeal through us" (2 Corinthians 5:20). Ambassadors are the official spokesmen of a sovereign power in a foreign state. Their word is backed up by the power that sent them out—but only when the word of the ambassador truly represents the mind and will of the sending state. So Christians everywhere are authorized spokesmen for God, "God making his appeal through us," but only when they are living authentically as Christians. Whenever that is true, God honors their word by making visible and realistic changes in the lives of those who respond to their witness. It is the mark of *undeniable reality* we saw in Chapter 2.

In John 20:22–23 the risen Lord Jesus gave his apostles (and us, through them) the authority to declare the forgiveness of sins or the retention of sins, depending on the response of listeners to the message of the gospel. To those who believe and accept, we may authoritatively declare, "Your sins are forgiven." To those who disbelieve, we have authority to say, "Your sins are yet retained."

This is part of that "priesthood of every believer" which Scripture teaches so clearly but which has been opposed by much of the institutional church through the centuries. Martin Luther recovered the truth briefly during the Reformation, but it was soon lost to sight again. Yet nothing is more encouraging to a servant of Christ than to see the Lord honoring his ministry by radical and permanent changes made in the people whose lives he touches.

The ministry of reconciliation is voluntarily accepted. "We implore you on Christ's behalf: Be reconciled to God" (2 Corinthians 5:20). Throughout this passage the apostle uses words that underscore the noncoercive nature of the gospel: "appeal," "beseech," "entreat." Since, as he says, we make our appeal "on behalf of Christ" or, literally, "in place of Christ," it is important that we be no more coercive than Jesus was when He ministered in the flesh on earth. In fact, authentic Christianity is Christ, by the Spirit, speaking through us today. It cannot be otherwise and still be of the Spirit. A remarkable absence of pressure characterizes the presentations Jesus made to people. He repeatedly offers Himself to them. He invites them to respond. He warns them of the consequences if they refuse. But He does not harangue them or use emotional stories to sway them. When they seem reluctant to respond, He neither prolongs the occasion nor makes the invitation easier. In fact, He is forever sending men away and thinning the ranks of His disciples.

As we have already noted, the proper approach to the servant of Christ is by the open statement of truth to commend ourselves to every man's conscience in the sight of God. Appeal is made to the will to respond, and if it does not do so, the matter is left with God to work further in His will and time. This is true not only for the evangelist, but also for the pastor-teacher or anyone who imparts the truth of the new covenant. "A man convinced against his will is of the same opinion still," says a wise old adage. Truth must find a willing response from the heart or it is of no value. Contrived responses are a waste of time.

The ministry of reconciliation achieves the impossible. "God made him who had no sin to be sin for us, so that in him we might become the righteousness of God" (2 Corinthians 5:21). Here is the supreme glory of the new covenant. It actually achieves what could never be achieved by fallen man: righteousness (worth) before a holy God! It seems impossible even for God. How can a God of justice justify the unjust? How can a righteous God righteously declare a sinner to be righteous? It is a puzzle that staggers the angels. But it was achieved! He who knew no sin, Jesus the righteous one, was made (on the cross) to be *sin* on behalf of us, who knew no righteousness, in order that the righteousness of God might be forever *ours!*

Righteousness is not only our unchanging *standing* before a holy God; it is also our present *state* whenever we are walking in the Spirit. The cross, therefore, is forever the ground of Satan's defeat. It was the ace up God's sleeve that Satan could not have anticipated. The great accuser can never find any ground by which he can turn a righteous God against us, for *all* our evil was forever cut off from us in the cross, and we now have a totally new identity. We are one spirit with Jesus Himself. "He who unites himself with the Lord is one with him in spirit" (1 Corinthians 6:17). No wonder Paul shouts in Romans 8:31: "If God is for us, who can be against us?" The inevitable outcome of righteousness is freedom. The righteous person is at rest; all his internal tensions and problems are solved. He is not anxious about himself but is free to give his attention to others. That is the glory of the new covenant. "If the Son sets you free, you will be free indeed" (John 8:36).

The ministry of reconciliation is experienced moment-by-moment. The opening verses of 2 Corinthians 6 continue the apostle's argument: "As God's fellow workers we urge you not to receive God's grace in vain. For he says, 'In the time of my favor I heard you, and in the day of salvation I helped you.' I tell you, now is the time of God's favor, now is the day of salvation" (2 Corinthians 6:1–2).

It is possible to accept the grace of God in vain. That is, it is possible to live much of life in dependence on the resources of the flesh rather than on the power and riches of the Spirit. Of course, for such moments or hours or days Christ has profited us nothing. We have Him, but we live as though He were not there. The grace and power of God are ours, but they do us no good.

Since we must take God's grace by faith (or dependence) and it comes to us moment-by-moment, then it is the present moment we must be concerned with. "I tell you, *now* is the time of God's favor, *now* is the day of salvation" (emphasis added). The fact that we walked in the Spirit a few moments ago is of no value to us now; the intention we have to walk in the Spirit in just a few more minutes does not redeem the present. If we choose to act in the flesh *now*, it is wasted time, gone forever, never to be retraced or regained. Let us run the race of life seeking to live each moment in the power and grace of the Spirit of Christ, for any time spent in the flesh is time in which we have accepted the grace of God in vain.

This, then, is the ministry of reconciliation that God has entrusted to us. He does not send us forth alone, but goes with us Himself to be both the Author and the Finisher of our faith. Perhaps it would help to summarize:

The Ministry of Reconciliation:
  Originates with God, not man;
  Is personally experienced;
  Is universally inclusive;
  Is without condemnation;
  Is delivered by men;
  Is owned and accredited by God;
  Is voluntarily accepted;
  Achieves what otherwise is impossible; and
  Is experienced moment-by-moment.

What a powerful and challenging opportunity His great ministry affords us! The apostle Paul can't help being caught up with the glory and wonder of it as he writes. He now closes this section of his letter dealing with the new covenant by relating his own experience of the ministry of reconciliation. He does so with incredible power and intense beauty. In doing so, he presents the story of his own life as Exhibit A.

Exhibit A

Mr. Smith sat in his attorney's office and began to lay out the case. "It all revolves around a verbal agreement between Mr. Johnson and myself," he explained. "We agreed to go into a business deal together, but we never set our agreement down in the form of a written contract. So my question to you is: Are verbal agreements binding?"

"Technically, yes," said the attorney. "According to the law, a verbal agreement is as binding as a written contract. The problem comes in proving that the verbal agreement actually took place. If one side denies that such a conversation ever took place, how does the other side prove it? For example, did either you or Mr. Johnson take any notes during your conversation when this agreement was made?"

"No," said Mr. Smith. "No notes were taken."

"Well, then," said the attorney, "were there any witnesses to the conversation?"

"None," replied Mr. Smith. "Mr. Johnson and I were the only persons present when the agreement was made."

"And, of course, I'm sure no recording was made of your conversation," said the attorney.

"Recording?" said Mr. Smith. "You mean, like this one?" He reached into his pocket and produced an audio cassette.

The attorney snatched it and held it up triumphantly. "You mean the entire conversation between you and Mr. Johnson is recorded on this tape? This is wonderful! This is Exhibit A! You have him right where you want him! We'll take him to court and *force* him to abide by your verbal agreement!"

Instead of joining in his attorney's enthusiasm, Mr. Smith hung his head in despair. "This is horrible!"

"Mr. Smith," said the attorney, "don't you understand? With this tape as Exhibit A, there's no way you can lose in court!"

"No, *you* don't understand!" Mr. Smith wailed. "That tape—Exhibit A, as you call it—is going to cost me thousands of dollars! I don't want to *enforce* the verbal agreement—I want to *get out* of it! That's a copy of a tape Mr. Johnson made of our conversation, and he's going to use it against me in court. Because of Exhibit A, there's no way I can win!"

When we think of the term "Exhibit A," we think of evidence that can't be denied, evidence that persuades and convicts, evidence that clinches the case. In this final chapter of our examination of authentic Christianity, we turn to Paul's "Exhibit A," his incontrovertible, incontestable, undeniable evidence for the validity of the new covenant, God's ironclad "verbal agreement" with the human race. The evidence Paul presents as Exhibit A is nothing less than the story of his own life.

We began this book with Paul's great declaration of his own experience of the new covenant: "Thanks be to

God, who always leads us in triumphal procession in Christ and through us spreads everywhere the fragrance of the knowledge of him" (2 Corinthians 2:14). Now we have come full circle, for the words with which we close are taken from the sixth chapter and are, likewise, the apostle Paul's own description of his experience in Christ. But note the difference. At the beginning of this account Paul spoke in glowing terms of the great principles he had found in Christ that governed and empowered his life. But here, at the end, he speaks more specifically of deeds and experiences and final results.

How we look to others

This is as it should be, for principle must always work itself out into practice. "Faith without deeds," says James, "is dead" (James 2:26). Thus an understanding of the new covenant that does not drastically alter the way of life is a useless thing. Paul's primary concern in this final section is to address the problem of communication with others who do not yet know this great secret of godlikeness, whether they are new Christians or still unregenerate. The new covenant cannot be lived in isolation but must bring us into contact with others, both Christians and non-Christians, because *authentic Christianity is designed for the world as it is*. Therefore, the apostle says: "We put no stumbling block in anyone's path, so that our ministry will not be discredited. Rather, as servants of God we commend ourselves in every way" (2 Corinthians 6:3–4).

Then Paul presents a most remarkable list of very practical ways by which the new covenant may be commended to others. We will look at this in some detail in a moment. But first, it may seem a contradiction for Paul to say here: "as servants of God we commend ourselves in every way," after he has said in 5:12, "We are not trying to commend ourselves to you again." The commendation he speaks of in chapter 5 is that of words: boastful self-commendation that seeks to impress others. Here in chapter 6 it is the commendation of deeds and attitudes that speak for themselves.

We shall look now at this impressive list to discover the right way Christians can commend themselves and the teaching of the new covenant to others:

> As servants of God we commend ourselves in every way: in great endurance; in troubles, hardships and distresses; in beatings, imprisonments and riots; in hard work, sleepless nights and hunger; in purity, understanding, patience and kindness; in the Holy Spirit and in sincere love; in truthful speech and in the power of God; with weapons of righteousness in the right hand and in the left; through glory and dishonor, bad report and good report; genuine, yet regarded as impostors (2 Corinthians 6:4–8).

The translators have obscured, in part, the divisions the apostle indicates in this paragraph. There are three major groupings of thought:

> In great endurance:
>   in troubles,
>   in hardships,
>   in distresses;
>
>   in beatings,
>   in imprisonments,
>   in riots;
>   in hard work,

in sleepless nights
in hunger;

By means of:
    purity,
    understanding,
    patience,
    kindness;

    the Holy Spirit,
    sincere love,
    truthful speech,
    the power of God;

With the weapons of righteousness:
    in the right hand and the left,
    in glory and dishonor,
    in bad report and good report.

It is obvious that the first group deals with the adverse pressures a Christian can encounter in life. The second group describes the character that must be displayed in the midst of these pressures. And the third group deals with the results produced, both good and apparently evil. And Paul fully exemplifies all these things! The apostles were pattern Christians, chosen to experience the full range of pressures and possibilities in order that we might have in them (and supremely in the Lord Jesus) an example to follow. It is not likely that we will be called upon to endure *all* these experiences, but we will surely be asked to endure *some* of them. Let us remember that the world around is watching us and only the manifestation of what Paul lists here will commend us to those who are watching our lives.

Endurance that endures

The key word to the first group is *endurance.* It means far more than simply toughing it out. Even non-Christians can endure hardness in that sense and some take great pride in their ability to do so. Athletes, marines, commandos, frontiersmen, and others often glory in their ability to confront hardship with fortitude and endurance. But this is not merely a reference to passive resignation that is content to wait with bowed head till the troubles have run their course.

The Greek word used here, *hupomone,* goes far beyond that. Rather, it is the courageous triumph that takes all the pressure and emerges with a cheer! It not only refuses to be broken by the pressure but is actually grateful for the opportunity to endure, knowing it will bring glory to God. "The apostles left the Sanhedrin, rejoicing because they had been counted worthy of suffering disgrace for the Name" (Acts 5:41).

Paul triumphantly endured everything on his list, often repeatedly. There were *afflictions* or, literally, "distresses." There were pressures that bore heavily upon his spirit—cares and intense anxieties that seldom let up in his life. There were *hardships*—the inescapable discomforts of life. And there were *calamities,* or to be more exact, "strictures," narrow places that seem to close one in on every side, offering no escape. In each of these circumstances the triumphant endurance produced by the new covenant commends Paul to those who are watching his life.

Next, there were troubles that stemmed directly from human opposition. There were *beatings* or *stripes.* Further on in this letter Paul says, "Five times I received from the Jews the forty lashes minus one. Three times I was beaten with rods, once I was stoned" (2 Corinthians 11:24–25). These painful beatings left their scars on him so that he could write to the Galatians, "Finally, let no one cause me trouble, for I bear on my body the marks of Jesus" (Galatians 6:17).

Often accompanying the beatings were *imprisonments*. Clement of Rome tells us the apostle was put into prison seven times, though only four of these are recorded in the Scriptures. At least two imprisonments were for more than two years, so Paul spent at least five years in prison and perhaps much more.

But that was not all. There were also *tumults*. This is a reference to the riots and mob violence that he sometimes provoked by the sweeping social changes his preaching produced. Perhaps nothing is more frightening than an angry mob, out of control, bent upon venting its rage on some hapless victim. But God enabled Paul to endure all of these encounters and trials with triumphant courage.

The last category of events calling for endurance involved, first, the *labors* he assumed. The word he uses here describes hard, unremitting toil, to the point of exhaustion. Paul doubtless spent many long hours at his tentmaking so he could present the gospel without charge! There were also *watchings*—sleepless nights, spent in prayer and meditation. These were not a matter of mere convenience to Paul but required grace and commitment. Then there was *hunger*. The reference is probably to periods of fasting, some deliberately chosen and some enforced upon him by the circumstances in which he found himself. These would take their toll of his physical and emotional strength, but through them all he was enabled to endure triumphantly.

The secret described

What was the secret of such endurance? It was never by a clenching of his fists, a jutting of his jaw, and a determination of his will to show the world how much he could take for Christ. Such an approach would soon have left even Paul broken and defeated, as he actually was in the early days of his Christian life. No, the secret of triumphant endurance was the new covenant— "everything coming from God, nothing coming from me"!

Paul possessed a certain kind of character that saw him through his troubles. It had to be invariable, or nearly so, for he never knew when it would be required. It consisted of four elements. First, there was *purity*. This refers to the careful avoidance of all sin that defiles or stains the flesh or spirit. Paul never allowed himself to be found in a compromising relationship with anyone. He carefully guarded not only his behavior, but his thought life, for he knew that is where defilement begins. Whenever he found himself toying with impurity, he immediately brought it to the Lord Jesus and obtained His cleansing and forgiveness.

Next there was *knowledge*. His mind was deliberately set upon truth, as he had learned it from the Scriptures and revelations of the Lord. He judged all persons and events, not from a human point of view, but from the divine viewpoint as revealed by the Spirit. The doctrine of Scripture was always his guide.

Third came *forbearance*. The Greek word, *macrothumia*, means patience, especially with regard to people. By nature Paul was impatient and hard driving. But he learned by the Spirit to wait for others to catch up, to be understanding about their weaknesses, and to wait quietly for the Lord to do the work of correction that was needed, for "to his own master he stands or falls" (Romans 14:4).

Finally, there was *kindness*. The original word has been described as meaning "the sympathetic kindliness or sweetness of temper that puts others at their ease and shrinks from giving pain." This attitude was to be shown without partiality, whether to a slave or to the emperor himself.

These four marks of Paul's character were what enabled him to endure. Anything other than momentary failure in any of them would have meant defeat. His pressures would have overwhelmed him, and he would have failed dismally to display that triumphant endurance that would commend him to the watching world.

Deeper yet
But there was something deeper even than these. The four characteristics of purity, knowledge, forbearance, and kindness were visible to other people. They lay in the realm of Paul's soul, his conscious experience in life. Deeper still, in the depths of his spirit, were the forces that undergirded and kept on making possible the display of the four characteristics just listed.

Behind everything else and at the root of it all was "the Holy Spirit." The third person of the Godhead is the gift of both the Father and the Son, serving as the guarantee of all else to come, dwelling permanently in Paul's heart, was the uncreated source of all that sustained Paul. It was the Spirit's constant delight to release to Paul at all times "the life of Jesus." Jesus Himself, by the Spirit, lived in Paul and upheld and empowered him, just as He lives in us and upholds us and empowers us through all our trials and tribulations. That "life of Jesus" invariably consists of three elements: love, truth, and power. This "life of Jesus" was continually supplied to Paul through the Spirit, explaining all that He was and did. This was the "sincere love," "truthful speech," and "the power of God" Paul talked about. No wonder he could handle life the way he did!

But Paul isn't through yet. Though the new covenant is designed to make us strong, it equips us *so that we might affect others.* There is always that watching world before which we must be commended! So Paul's final category speaks of the effect of "the weapons of righteousness." He sees the worth and value he has in God's eyes—worth and value that is based on the righteousness of Christ, not any righteousness of his own—as a kind of sword or spear by which we attack the forces of darkness. With these weapons, we set free those who have been held bondage by Satan. Hence, the term "weapons of righteousness." Righteousness, here, is a summary term gathering up the four distinctives Paul listed in the previous section: purity, understanding, patience, and kindness. These four "weapons of righteousness" have a powerful effect on others in two ways:

First, such righteousness affects both "the right hand and the left." This saying probably goes back to Jesus' statement in the Sermon on the Mount: "Do not let your left hand know what your right hand is doing" (Matthew 6:3). By this He refers to the public and private life. The right hand is the public life, the left hand is the private. Thus, the effect of a righteous life will touch both the public actions of others (their social relationships) and their private lives as well (changing their attitudes). True Christianity does not make superficial changes—it changes people within and without.

Second, the effect of such change is also twofold: "in honor and dishonor." Those freed by Christ will be placed in varying positions before the world. Some will occupy positions of honor, such as Manaen, a member of the court of Herod, the tetrarch, mentioned in Acts 13, and Sergius Paulus, the converted Roman proconsul described in the same chapter. Others will be obscure men and women about whom the world knows or cares nothing. But even these will find a varying acceptance. Some will be of "bad report" and others will be of "good report." Jesus Himself had predicted this: "Remember the words I spoke to you: 'No servant is greater than his master.' If they persecuted me, they will persecute you also" (John 15:20). But, whether honored by the world, or dishonored; whether held in good or bad esteem, all are equally loved and owned by God, all are equally empowered by the Spirit (if they choose to draw upon Him), and all are expected to live before the world in such a way as to commend the gospel to all people.

The paradoxical Christian

In his book *That Incredible Christian*, A.W. Tozer describes some of the many paradoxes one finds in authentic Christianity—and in authentic Christians:

> At the heart of the Christian system lies the cross of Christ with its divine paradox. The power of Christianity appears in its antipathy toward, never in its agreement with, the ways of fallen men. The truth of the cross is revealed in its contradictions. . . . Simply observe the true Christian as he puts into practice the teachings of Christ and His apostles. Note the contradictions:
>
> The Christian believes that in Christ he has died, yet he is more alive than before and he fully expects to live forever. He walks on earth while seated in heaven and though born on earth he finds that after his conversion he is not at home here. . . . He loses his life to save it and is in danger of losing

it if he attempts to preserve it. He goes down to get up. If he refuses to go down he is already down, but when he starts down he is on his way up.

He is strongest when he is weakest and weakest when he is strong. Though poor he has the power to make others rich, but when he becomes rich his ability to enrich others vanishes. He has most after he has given most away and has least when he possesses most.

He may be and often is highest when he feels lowest and most sinless when he is most conscious of sin. He is wisest when he knows that he knows not and knows least when he has acquired the greatest amount of knowledge. He sometimes does most by doing nothing and goes furthest when standing still. In heaviness he manages to rejoice and keeps his heart glad even in sorrow. . . .

He fears God but is not afraid of Him. In God's presence he feels overwhelmed and undone, yet there is nowhere he would rather be than in that presence. He knows that he has been cleansed from his sin, yet he is painfully conscious that in his flesh dwells no good thing.

He loves supremely One whom he has never seen, and though himself poor and lowly he talks familiarly with One who is King of all kings and Lord of all lords, and is aware of no incongruity in so doing. He feels that he is in his own right altogether less than nothing, yet he believes without question that he is the apple of God's eye and that for him the Eternal Son became flesh and died on the cross of shame. . . .

Incredible Christian!

[A. W. Tozer, *That Incredible Christian* (Wheaton IL: Tyndale House, special edition, undated), pp. 11–13.]

These words of A. W. Tozer echo and expand upon the series of magnificent paradoxes Paul describes in his depiction of the authentic Christian in 2 Corinthians 6:8–10. He says that he and his fellow authentic Christians are

> genuine, yet regarded as impostors; known, yet regarded as unknown; dying, and yet we live on; beaten, and yet not killed; sorrowful, yet always rejoicing; poor, yet making many rich; having nothing, and yet possessing everything.

Clearly, authentic Christians present an enigma to the world, because their lives consist of a series of paradoxes. Only the man or woman who stands poised between two worlds can qualify for such a description. The authentic Christian is in a highly vulnerable position, stretched between God and man. We must be content to be called imposters by some, to be thought of as unknown, to be threatened and punished, to be poor and have nothing—all the while knowing that, before God, the very reverse is true! As God sees us, we are his true children, known to all heaven, living and rejoicing in the spirit when the flesh is perishing, ever imparting the unsearchable riches of Christ to many, and being heirs of all creation when time trembles into eternity.

Is it not fitting, therefore, that the apostle should close this great discourse with an earnest appeal, rising out of the depths of his heart:

> We have spoken freely to you, Corinthians, and opened wide our hearts to you. We are not withholding our affection from you, but you are withholding yours from us. As a fair exchange—I speak as to my children—open wide your hearts also (2 Corinthians 6:11–13).

Love, truth, and power all require response to be fully operative. Each will grow to infinite expansion if it is met by faith, though it be as small as a grain of mustard seed. Paul was not holding anything back from the Corinthians. He had opened his heart to them and told them everything he had learned from the Lord. Their present weakness was due to only one thing: a failure to respond to the truth they knew—a reluctance to act on what they had been told. So his appeal comes as a father to his children: "Open wide your hearts!"

The present low state of the church in the world is surely due to the same cause. Christians do not really believe what they sing about and profess. They have lost the consciousness of the greatness of God and his ability to act today. Dr. D. Martyn Lloyd-Jones, noted pastor of Westminster Chapel in London, England, has made an appeal similar to that of Paul's:

> I speak especially to those of us who are Evangelicals. We must not continue with our religious life and methods precisely as if nothing were happening round and about us, and as if we were still living in the spacious days of peace. We have loved certain methods. And how delightful they were! What could be more enjoyable than to have and to enjoy our religion in the form with which we have for so long been familiar? How enjoyable just to sit and listen. What an intellectual and perhaps also emotional and artistic treat.

> But alas! How entirely unrelated to the world in which we live it has often been! How little has it had to offer to men and women who have never known our background and our kind of life, who are entirely ignorant of our very idiom

and even our presuppositions. But in any case how detached and self-contained, how removed from a world that is seething in trouble with the foundations of everything that has been most highly prized rocking and shaking.

[D. Martyn Lloyd-Jones, *The Plight of Man and the Power of God*, p. 11.]

What possibilities lie before us as Christians if only we are worthy of them! How little the world realizes the treasure that lies in its midst in the church of Jesus Christ. But how little the church realizes it, too. Think of what 300 million "qualified ministers of the new covenant" could accomplish around the world if they began to function as Paul lived. I invite you, as you close this book, to bow your knees before the Father of our Lord Jesus Christ, and in His name, pray: "Father, make me a qualified minister of the new covenant. Open my eyes to the full meaning of the truth that Jesus lives in me, by the Spirit. Make me hunger and thirst after His righteousness, so that according to your promise I might be filled. Amen."

NOTE TO THE READER

The publisher invites you to share your response to the message of this book by writing Discovery House Publishers, Box 3566, Grand Rapids, MI 49501, USA. For information about other Discovery House books, music, or videos, contact us at the same address or call 1-800-653-8333. Find us on the Internet at http://www.dhp.org/ or send e-mail to books@dhp.org.